D1105077

The Itinerary of Benjamin of Tudela

The Itinerary of
Benjamin of Tudela

TRAVELS IN THE MIDDLE AGES

Introductions by

MICHAEL A. SIGNER, 1983

MARCUS NATHAN ADLER, 1907

A. ASHER, 1840

Joseph Simon Pangloss Press

MALIBU, CALIFORNIA

Second Printing, 1987

Published by Joseph Simon/Pangloss Press
P.O. Box 4071, Malibu, California 90265

Library of Congress Cataloging in Publication Data

Benjamin, of Tudela, 12th cent.
 The itinerary of Benjamin of Tudela.

 Translation of Masa'ot shel Rabi Binyamin.
 Bibliography: p. 155
 1. Benjamin, of Tudela, 12th cent. 2. Voyages and travels. 3. Jews—Social life and customs—Early works to 1800. I. Title.
G370.B5B46 1983   910.4   83-17486
 ISBN 0-934710-07-4
 ISBN 0-934710-06-6 (lim. ed.)

CONTENTS

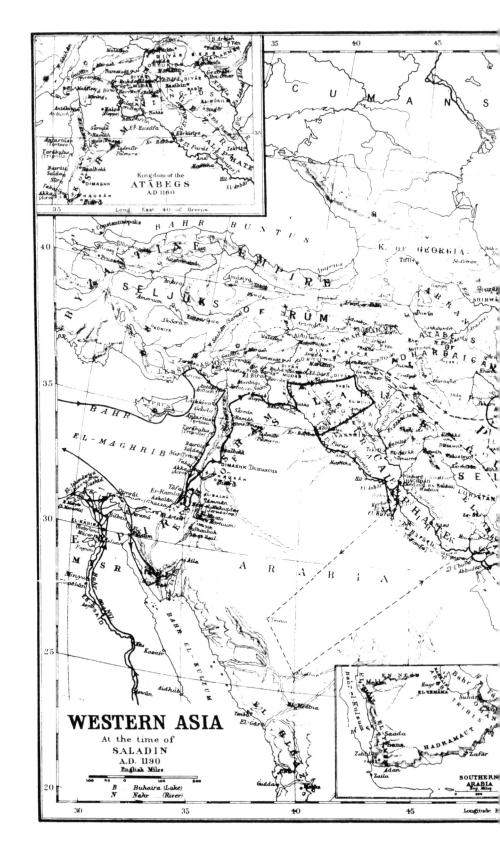

Kingdom of the
ATĀBEGS
A.D. 1160

WESTERN ASIA

At the time of
SALADIN
A.D. 1190
English Miles

B   Buhaira (Lake)
N   Nahr   (River)

SOUTHERN
ARABIA

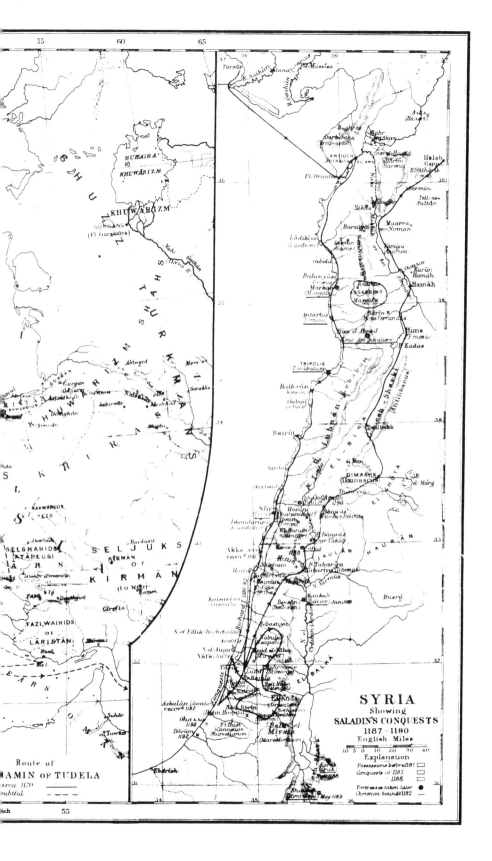

SYRIA
Showing
SALADIN'S CONQUESTS
1187–1190
English Miles

10 5 0 10 20 30 40

Explanation

Possessions before 1187
Conquests of 1187
1188
Fortresses taken later ●
Christian bound.ᵈ 1192

Route of
...AMIN of TUDELA
...rca 1170
...ubtful

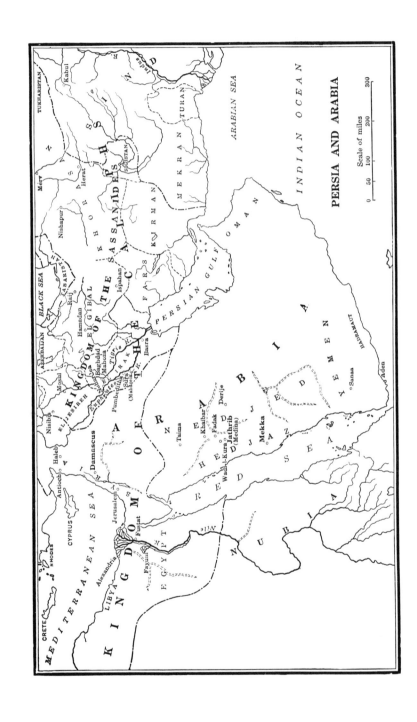

PERSIA AND ARABIA

Scale of miles
0   50   100   200   300

The Itinerary of Benjamin of Tudela

Introductions by

MICHAEL A. SIGNER, 1983

MARCUS NATHAN ADLER, 1907

A. ASHER, 1840

SIGNER INTRODUCTION

OST PEOPLE consider the Middle Ages as an historical period which was punctuated by moments of barbarian violence with counterpoints of contemplative chants of monks. For modern Jews the Middle Ages have provided a portrait of persecution and exile contrasted with the continuity of religious study. In the larger scheme of European history which serves as the background to the cultural and political institutions of our own era the Middle Ages have become a period utterly set apart, concentrating upon the spiritual, the etherial, and the superstitious.

The *Itinerary of Benjamin of Tudela* illuminates the shadowy pictures which we have constructed of the Middle Ages. With Benjamin as our guide we will find that our mental maps of the medieval world require expanded horizons. Southern France, Italy, Greece, and the Holy Land blend with the exotic realms of unknown Tibet, China, and India. We will visit with Byzantine emperors, caliphs and kings, together with wild tribes of "Assassins," and pearl fishermen on the Indian Ocean. The Crusaders, and their exploits in the Levant, pale before the warfare of the Persian king with the Turkish tribes. Benjamin's Jewish hosts along the way are more than students of sacred Jewish lore. They are traders, dyers, tanners—and many Jews are warriors who lived by plunder and conquest.

The *Itinerary* makes the view that medieval religion was monolithic untenable. Christianity may have presented itself as a unity under the papacy, in the treatises of twelfth-century theologians, but Benjamin revealed to his reader a world of Byzantine Christians, of Jacobites and Nestorians. In the world of Islam we encounter the Caliph of Baghdad, who is the "Protector of the Faithful," and the "Protector of the Faithful" in Cairo, who sets his authority against the supreme Caliph in Baghdad. Benjamin saw contrasting communities of Jews as well: the *Epikursim* on Cypress, the black Jews of India, "who know Moses and the Prophets and to a small extent Talmud and Halachah;" and the two communities of Alexandria who read the weekly portion in the Five Books of Moses according to entirely different lectionary cycles. Religion was diverse and dynamic in Benjamin's world.

Benjamin's curiosity was not restricted by religious or sectarian exclusivism. He was as curious about architecture as he was about manufacturing processes. Non-Jewish religious practices were meticulously recorded, and the more exotic they were the more details we find. He describes in great detail the burial practices and worship patterns of pagans in the Indian Ocean. The diet of the Oghuz Turks or Tartars becomes an occasion for a description of an exotic people. People and their forms of governance receive careful attention.

The diversity of Benjamin's interests and his broad scope of narrative do not blur his focus. Although he is interested primarily in Jews, Benjamin's Jews exist within the context of their larger civilization. It is the peculiar merit of Benjamin's *Itinerary* to view Jews as part of their environments rather than in contrast to their environments. He does not write an apologetic for the superiority of Judaism over the world in which the Jews lived. Rather, he narrates parallels between Jews and their hosts, attempting to highlight the equality of Jews with their neighbors. Benjamin is interested in all Jews: their livelihood, their modes of self-governance, their relationship to power, and their religious life. Judaism becomes a portion of the total identity of the communities he visited. His all-encompassing view of the Jews whom he visited makes the *Itinerary* a precious document about medieval Jewry.

A unique document would suggest a unique author. Who was Benjamin ben (son of) Jonah of Tudela? What was the intellectual milieu which trained his eye? What message did he hope to communicate to the reader of his *Itinerary*? Finally, what interested two translators in the nineteenth century to produce translations of his work. These questions form the framework of the introduction to the journey which took place nearly eight hundred years ago.

The World of Benjamin of Tudela

THE ITINERARY is the only remaining work authored by Benjamin. We must rely upon it for all the information we can glean about its author. Benjamin remains quite aloof throughout the entire narrative of the *Itinerary*, and rarely punctuates his observations with biographical information. The only indication we have is the identification with the city of Tudela in Navarre, which is in northern Spain.

A reading to the Hebrew text of the *Itinerary* reveals more about Benjamin. He writes in a rather formal medieval Hebrew. His Hebrew is suffused with Arabic forms. This would certainly indicate that Benjamin knew Arabic. It was probably his mother tongue. Arabic gave Benjamin the linguistic key to the world he set out to explore in Asia and Africa. Benjamin's knowledge of Arabic also opens up a path toward a deeper understanding of his intellectual milieu.

Both the literary form and language of Benjamin's work indicate that he was the inheritor of a cultural tradition which derived from *al-Andalus*, or Moslem Spain. The political unity which characterized the Iberian peninsula during the tenth and eleventh centuries was shaken during the first half of the twelfth century. From the north came Christian knights engaged in a crusade or *Reconquista*. It was their desire to recapture the Iberian peninsula and restore it to Christian rule. North Africa was the home of Berber tribes which disturbed the political and religious atmosphere of southern Spain. Unlike their Moslem ancestors who came to Spain in the seventh century, the Berber tribes believed in a strict ascetic observance of Islamic theology. Their intolerance for religious minorities such as Christians or Jews sent waves of migration in different directions. The raids by the Almohades at mid-century sent Jews to Cordova in northern Spain, to Provence, and to Egypt. All of these countries were part of Benjamin's route. We may assume, therefore, that Benjamin was part of the same cultural and intellectual tradition which formed the great Jewish philosopher, Moses Maimonides (1135–1205), who fled Spain for Egypt.

Iberian Jewry had a long and proud cultural tradition. Its roots were set during the Roman empire, and Jews were evident throughout the successor kingdom to the Romans—the Visigoths. Chronicles and church literature indicate that Jews were active throughout Spain in diverse economic ventures under the Visigoths. With the invasion and conquest of the Moslems, which began in 711, Jews became a part of a unique cultural and political life.

The development of Arabic culture through translations of classical Greek works in physics, mathematics, astronomy, metaphysics, medicine, and ethics was one of the most remarkable aspects of the development of world culture. These translations were augmented by Arabic commentaries on the classics as well as original scientific work in Arabic. In the area of *belles lettres* there was a flowering of works in poetry and prose. Science and art flourished. Jews eagerly absorbed these new cultural developments.

Benjamin grew to maturity in two cultural worlds: the world of Arabic science and culture; and the world of Jewish culture which encompassed the Bible, and the classical works of the rabbis, as they appeared in the Talmud and Midrash. The *Itinerary* provides no direct evidence that he knew philosophy, but his intellectual curiosity about the diverse religious philosophies which he encountered suggest that he was familiar with the questions which interested philosophers. Benjamin did know his Bible, and the *Itinerary* demonstrates that he chose his words carefully to provide hints to his reader that more than one meaning might apply to a particular situation. On several occasions Benjamin cites scriptural texts to indicate that what he observed appeared to fulfill the meaning of the biblical phrase.

It would be difficult to determine the extent of Benjamin's knowledge of rabbinic literature based upon a single document. The *Itinerary* suggests that he was very interested in the forms of schooling in Talmud that occurred throughout the world. Benjamin also seemed to know enough rabbinic lore to be able to determine what was normative rabbinic belief and practice.

The scope of interests revealed in the *Itinerary* indicates that Benjamin belonged to a group of Andalusian Jews who valued the synthesis of Islamic and Jewish cultures. They viewed themselves as an intellectual and social elite. Among these Jews both intellect and family ancestry were highly valued. They were expected to be able to compose Arabic poetry and to discourse on philosophic topics. Erudition in rabbinic literature was evidenced in many of the treatises they composed.

Beyond intellectual accomplishment, these Jews were expected to provide service to the Jewish community. They were to provide for the maintenance of charitable institutions to support the needy. Philanthropy, however, went beyond making personal wealth available to the community. The Jews of al-Andalus had become influential in the complex network of kingdoms and caliphates which governed the districts of the Iberian peninsula. They served as advisors to Christian and Moslem rulers alike. They gathered taxes and performed other bureaucratic services. Twelfth-century Andalusian Jews used their influence to intervene with the ruling elite to ameliorate the status of their fellow Jews.

This unique combination of piety, erudition, and power had developed over a two hundred year period in Spain. In the tenth century the Abbasid caliph in Spain had Hasdai Ibn Shaprut as his trusted advisor. Ibn Shaprut was a skilled diplomat and negotiator who took part in the complex net of alliances between the Spanish caliph, Byzantine emperor, and Charlemagne of Europe. The Abbasid caliphate in Spain was supported in its claims of independence from Baghdad by these alliances. We have correspondence from Hasdai which indicates that within the larger context of international negotiation, he intervened on behalf of the Jewish communities. Utilizing the power of his office he sought to bring relief to Jews in other lands who felt the "yoke of exile." Hasdai also initiated correspondence with the Khazars, the tribes who lived between Islam and Christianity, which had converted to Judaism. Scholars have debated the authenticity of these letters. However, the curiosity about a powerful kingdom whose ruler identified with Judaism would fit into the context of Ibn Shaprut's international diplomatic efforts on behalf of his brethren.

Jewish military power was not exclusively to be sought in distant lands. Twelfth-century Spanish Jews could look back one hundred years to the life of Samuel Ibn Nagrella of Granada. Ibn Nagrella was a military leader who led the armies of the Emir of Granada. He recorded his military victories in poetry, and imagined himself as King David. His poems indicate that he felt destined, like David, to lead his people to victory and safety. Ibn Nagrella was more than a soldier-poet. He composed treatises on

Biblical studies and wrote an important methodological study of Talmudic argumentation. His life and writings received special attention from Benjamin's contemporary, Abraham Ibn Daud, whose *Book of Tradition* chronicled the men of virtue among Spanish Jewry.

Benjamin could indeed look back upon men of broad vision. His own generation, although shaken by invasions, found stability. Their stability did not make them parochial or insular. They engaged in the Mediterranian commerce which flourished during the twelfth century. For many years Benjamin's *Itinerary* was the sole witness to the vast and diverse trade on the Mediterranian and Indian Oceans. During the past fifty years many letters from merchants have been discovered and translated. Those documents, although emanating from Egypt, belong to the same universe of discourse as the *Itinerary*.

The letters of these merchants augment the *Itinerary*. Benjamin describes the merchandise in various ports. The *Itinerary* does not tell us about the dangers of pirates and robbers which constantly plagued the ships and caravans of merchants.

Despite substantial wealth, many traders led solitary lives. They complained of their loneliness, of their inability to negotiate the complex of government taxes, and of the meticulous care needed to preserve their "good name," or reputation. If these traders had been Benjamin's hosts or travelling companions we know that he would have been able to speak with them about the prices of gems; the enormous instability of markets in various spices; and the negotiating procedures with merchants from different ethnic backgrounds and languages. Benjamin's merchant companions would have travelled only six days during the week. Each Sabbath, or Saturday, they would have rested and prayed. It appears that a pious religious life was of paramount importance in establishing the trust which held mercantile relationships together.

Benjamin journeyed through a world which was a mosaic of political configurations. If his companions were merchants, his concerns were different. The *Itinerary* is silent about the difficulties he encountered on the way. All we learn is the distance between communities. He tells us about his journeys by ship, so that we can assume that he made the balance of his travels over land. His perceptions of cities, people, and monuments were shaped by the world in which he was educated. Piety, poetry, and power shaped his vision. His narrative of the journey reveals a unique perception.

Benjamin the Traveller

THE ROADS between East and West were well worn by the second half of the twelfth century. Benjamin's travels between 1169–1171 occurred during a period of relative calm. Northern Europe was evolving into a series of stable monarchies. The papacy in Rome was advancing a vision of Christian unity which extended beyond the geographic borders of Europe. Christian kingdoms existed as independent islands in Syria and Palestine. The Iberian peninsula saw Christian monarchs established in regions which had been under Islamic control for hundreds of years. The impulse to spread the banner of Christ continued as new calls for a third Crusade to the Holy land would be issued within a decade of Benjamin's journay. Islam was an enemy for its sovereignty over places held sacred by Christians.

For people in the Middle Ages the sovereignty over sacred places was most important. They lived in an enchanted world. Forests, abandoned buildings, and ruins were inhabited by demons and evil spirits. Relics of saints and sites of shrines were places in which miraculous healings took place. A sudden reversal of a person's fate such as recovery from an illness might evoke a vow to make a journey to a place of pilgrimage and offer thanks.

During the age of Benjamin Christian pilgrims made their way along the rivers of France and the Pyrenees mountains to the Church at Campostella to visit the shrine of St. James. The Holy Land and Syria attracted many Christian pilgrims. Jews also travelled to Palestine. As Benjamin relates his journey, their focus was the Galilee with its tombs of rabbinic scholars or the tombs of the biblical patriarchs in Hebron.

Islam also evoked pilgrimages to holy sites. One of the pillars of Islam is the *Hadj* or pilgrimage to Mecca. However, the pilgrimage to sites related to holy figures in the Old and New Testaments was also frequent. Moslems are frequent worshippers in many of the sites described in the *Itinerary*. Reports from Christian missionaries in the Middle East indicate the Moslems easily mixed with Christians at holy sites in Palestine. This confluence of religious pilgrims would seem to contrast with the harsh rhetoric of each religion. It is well to remember that the faithful do not always heed the admonitions of their religious leaders. The need to seek the intervention of a sainted person overcame the barriers of separated traditions.

Benjamin was not alone on his journeys. Merchants, pilgrims, and simply restless souls had taken to the road in a world which afforded the opportunity, despite risks, to move. He carefully records people, places and objects which were part of these worlds.

The delicate peace which prevailed through the countries of Benjamin's journey was in counterpoint to sudden wars and pillage. The *Itinerary* records fortifications: In Genoa and Pisa the households have turrets and are prepared for fighting. Naples has fortifications which were built during the biblical period. Salerno has walls on the land side and the sea on the other. The walls which surround the city of Jerusalem are thick, and the Jews dwell near the Tower of David, which is the strongest part of the wall.

Military preparedness is a corollary of physical fortification. The

Itinerary narrates the warlike virtues of the Kofar-al-Turak or Oghuz Turkish tribe. In the Balkans and throughout the reaches of Persia are people prepared to fight wars. Benjamin is particularly interested in groups of Jews which were in a state of military strength. People in Tadmor, Khaibar, and India are described as valiant men of war. Military alliances between Jews and fierce tribes are part of a global vision of Jews who can establish and maintain themselves as a part of the world population.

Military weakness also motivates alliances. Benjamin reports an alliance of this nature between the Byzantines and their mercenaries. The *Itinerary* shares the European and Islamic pejorative image of the Byzantines as flaccid and effeminate.

Sovereignty and forms of government become a focus for Benjamin's observations. He shared the ignorance of many of his fellow Spanish Jews about forms of government north of the Pyrenees. The Pope is considered the head of the entire kingdom of Edom (Christianity). We do not find the name of any European sovereign in the *Itinerary*. Beginning with Constantinople, however, the names of monarchs begin to appear. Despite the decline of the Abbasid caliphate in Baghdad, with respect to its international sovereignty, there is a lengthy description of the palace and its properties. The caliph is portrayed as an absolute tyrant who keeps all members of his family under house arrest. His absolute power is augmented by the symbolic rituals of his public reading of the Quran and the retinue which surrounds him.

Benjamin discerns sovereignty in forms beyond the monarchies which were familiar to him. He describes the power of the "Old Man of the Assassins;" the Turkish tribes have their unique leaders; and he notes the amazing power which the priests of Ceylon have over their people.

With rare exceptions Benjamin does not evaluate these forms of governance—he reports them. The priests of Ceylon hold their power by "trickery and witchcraft" which confirms people "in their error." In the Fatimid kingdom of Egypt he records the Emir al-Muminin, the Protector of the Faithful, who rose up against the Abbasid caliph; and "between these two parties there is a lasting feud." Governing powers may have absolute power over their subjects, but no single power seems to have absolute power over all peoples. This principle is most important for Benjamin, as we shall see that it is an important basis for his world view.

The *Itinerary* maintains a parallel track throughout with respect to Jewish sovereignty. In the communities of southern France, Italy, Greece, and Palestine he records the names of three individuals from each community. We might presume that these three men represented the *Bet-Din* or ecclesiastical court of the Jews. These religious courts had a tradition of autonomy which originated in the Jewish communities of Palestine during late antiquity. Their rulings over both civil and personal legal matters were authoritative in the community. The only course of appeal was directly to the community itself during the worship service. During the twelfth century even this source of appeal was curtailed. In addition to the *Bet-Din* each community had administrators who looked after the charitable funds. These men received honorific titles such as *Parnas* (Warden) or *Rosh* (Leading Man). We do not know how long the individuals remained in office, but there is strong indication that these duties were carried out by members of the same family. Benjamin's lists of communal leaders indicates that many were related by marriage.

When Benjamin narrates his travels among the Jews in Damascus, Baghdad and beyond, the lists of communal elders diminish. This would coincide with the traditions of the Middle Eastern communities which held a more hierarchic mode of government. In several communities we meet individuals with the honorific title *Nasi* or "Prince." This title seems to indicate that its bearer ascribed his family lineage to the house of King David. The function of these men was governance of the community. They had no peers or co-regents.

In Syria, Iraq, and Egypt Benjamin describes the Heads of the Academy, or *Gaonim*. It might seem unusual that the head of an institution devoted to study would have significant governing power. The academies, however, were more than scholastic institutions. They had legislative power comparable to the schools of Islamic jurisprudence. The *Gaon* had the power to appoint rabbis and judges in all the communities under the jurisdiction of the caliph. Even under the diminished power of the Abbasid caliphate, during the twelfth century, Jewish communities deferred to the *Gaonim*. Each academy could trace its lineage back to the period of Persian rule in the fourth and fifth centuries. As Benjamin indicates, they were confirmed in their power by the Islamic rulers, "going back to the time of Mohammed."

The importance of lineage may be seen in Benjamin's insistence that *Gaonim* trace their ancestry back both to the Levites and to Moses. According to Benjamin's description the *Gaonim* were not elected, but part of a hierarchy which led to becoming *Gaon*. We learn this from his elaboration of titles such as "fifth" or "seventh" in the order of succession to the *Gaon*.

Another account of the powers and privileges of the *Gaonim*, written prior to the *Itinerary*, by Nathan the Babylonian, for the community of Kairwan in North Africa, corroborates Benjamin's description of their power. Nathan the Babylonian indicates that the *Gaonim* were elected to office, and that fierce rivalries during the tenth century led to the weakening of the powers of the office.

The *Itinerary* notes that many communities in Persia, which were not under the rule of the caliph, had their rabbis appointed by the *Gaonim*. Benjamin describes *Gaonim* in both Damascus and Baghdad. In Cairo he relates that two congregations have loyalties to different *Gaonim*. Egyptian Jewry also had its own supreme religious officer, the "Prince of Princes," who was appointed over the communities in Egypt. His power to appoint rabbis for all these communities would place him equal in function, if not honor, to the *Gaonim*.

The most elaborate description of Jewish self-government is reserved for the Head of the Exile (the Exilarch). He is a descendant of King David, and possesses a complete pedigree of his lineage. The Emir al-Muminin invests him with authority over all the communities under Islamic sovereignty. Mohammed himself ordered that every Jew or Moslem should stand up and salute him. A triumphal march through the streets of Baghdad each Thursday precedes his meeting with the caliph at the royal palace. This pomp and glory demonstrates to Benjamin's satisfaction that the biblical prophecy, "The scepter shall not depart from Judah, nor the ruler's staff between his feet; so that tribute shall come to him and the homage of peoples be his." (Gen. 49:10) The Head of the Exile, like the caliph, is a man of property, and bestows charity and benevolence upon his people.

The narrative of the *Itinerary* is more than a travelogue. Even descriptions of monuments are often given with an eye toward past imperial glory. Benjamin gives careful attention to remnants of Israel's past in Palestine. He also records the ruins which were ascribed to shadowed figures in the Bible. We know little about King Jeconiah, who was taken in captivity by the Babylonian king in 590 B.C.E., yet his palace is recorded by Benjamin. Ezra and Daniel are hardly significant figures in the total narrative of the Bible, yet they are the objects of veneration by both caliph and Persian king. In order to truly understand why Benjamin would record these monuments with such precision we need to understand the theme which underlies the *Itinerary*: the continued existence of Israel as a scattered people.

Mobility and Stability:
Benjamin's Hidden Formula for the Continuity of the Jewish People

THREE MOTIVATIONS have been suggested for Benjamin's journey. First is *Aliyah*, a Hebrew word which literally means to "go up" to the land of Israel. Benjamin was part of the pilgrims who went to pray at the relics of the past, or render thanks to God for favors received. Another motivation derives from the political instability in the Iberian peninsula during the second half of the twelfth century. He wanted to know, as Adler put it, "where would his expatriated brethren find asylum." A third motive may have been his desire to set forth a record of the many prosperous mercantile communities.

A cursory reading of the *Itinerary* would validate all of these motivations. Yet neither piety nor mercantile interests explains the broad scope of Benjamin's journey. Medieval authors rarely set down their thoughts without some didactic or edifying motive. Benjamin of Tudela was no exception. If we look beyond his curiosity about technology or forms of pagan worship we discover that he was far from random in his choice of subjects to describe.

Aside from other motivations, the *Itinerary of Benjamin of Tudela* represents a contribution to the literature of consolation for the Jewish people. What consolation did medieval Jews require? The answer is rooted in the biblical narrative which provided the vocabulary for Jewish expression. Essentially, the biblical narrative of the Old Testament describes a dialectic of the people of Israel in the land of Palestine, and outside the land of Palestine. The land was part of the covenant between the patriarch Abraham who made a covenant with God. As surety for Abraham's faith God promised him a continuity of Jewish descendants which would be as numerous as the stars in the heavens or the sands upon the shore. These descendants would inherit the land of Israel in perpetuity. The people of Israel depart Egypt and make a covenant with God at Sinai to bring them into the "promised land." Much of the later biblical narrative relates the difficulties of Israel's failure to live up to its covenant with God. The prophetic literature presents the dilemma of exile from the land, set against the firm knowledge and hope that God would restore the people to its land.

The final books of the Hebrew canonized Scripture—Ezra, Nehemiah, I and II Chronicles, relate the restoration of the children of Israel in their land under the benevolence of Cyrus of Persia (539 B.C.E.). Scripture thereby becomes an imaginative blueprint for the hope of Israel's restoration. In the wake of the destruction of the Temple by the Romans in the year 70 C.E. the rabbis quickly seized this blueprint. Their legal system, biblical exegesis, and prayer service, were created upon the assumption that God would return the scattered remnant of Israel to its land. Their vision was so fixed on the hope of return that they did little to record the history and achievements of the diaspora communities. The massive literature of the Babylonian and Palestinean Talmud do little to illumine the life of those communities or to explicate the interrelationships with non-Jewish governments.

Rabbinic literature became a code which obfuscated the non-Jewish world. Rome was identified with Biblical Edom; Ishmael became the code for Arabic nations, or Islam. Adherents of non-Jewish religions were called "idolators." These code words for the non-Jewish world had behavioral consequences. In order to observe rabbinic law Jews were urged to separate from non-Jews. The exclusivism and triumphalism of the post-Constantine (fourth century) church was matched by an internal exclusivism for Jews. This exclusivism was based on the hope that God would eventually send his deliverer, a descendant of the biblical King

David, to save the Jewish people. This hope provided consolation for the Jews.

Political reality must have made this hope seem very dim for medieval Jewry. Christian theologians raised the question of how long God would continue to love Israel in its exile. How much better, they reasoned, to accept that the Egyptian exile had lasted four hundred years and the Babylonian exile had lasted the same length of time. By the eleventh century it had been nearly one thousand years of exile. Was this not a sign to the Jews that they ought to give up the hope of return?

The culture of Islamic Spain presented the problem of exile in more subtle ways. The flowering of Arabic culture in the sciences, philosophy, and theology was not without its theological triumphalism. Moslems believed that the Arabic language was the highest form of divine revelation. Their military conquests were supported by cultural development. History and geography were not abstractions for training the mind, but modes of discourse which presented the triumph of Islam all over the world. The measured tones of Arab historians, theologians, and geographers were harmonized with the song of Allah's victory.

The mid-twelfth century presented a cultural crisis to Jews in Spain. Christians and Moslems were at war, both in Spain and in the Middle East. Neither side had yet won a definitive victory. The Berber invaders brought an end to the comfortable life in Granada; and the courtyards of Cordoba, and other cities, brought no rest and no return. No direction seemed to provide comfort.

Consolation for Israel, living in Spain, came in genres of literature which had not previously been part of Jewish religious lore. Judah HaLevi, a poet who had been educated in the twelfth-century cultural ambiance of al-Andalus, rejected the life of Spain and moved to Palestine. Recent biographers of HaLevi tend to account for his change of heart by placing his departure within the context of his belief that only in the land of Israel could one fully receive divine revelation. This revelation would enable him to understand when deliverance would come to Israel. Much of HaLevi's rejection of the cultural synthesis of Jewish and Islamic learning is to be found in his book, *The Kuzari: A Defense of the Despised Faith*. The *Kuzari* rejected the hope that true knowledge could be obtained only by the force of reason. True hope resided in a return to the land of Israel.

While Judah HaLevi utilized a philosophic dialogue to attack the cultural climate in Spain, his younger contemporary, Abraham Ibn Daud of Toledo, wrote history to defend it. His *Book of Tradition* indicated that Spain was the rightful inheritor of the authority of Moses, the Prophets, the Rabbis, and the *Gaonim*. To supplement the argument that God's consolation for the Jews would begin in Spain, Ibn Daud composed a chronicle about Jewish life during the Second Commonwealth in Palestine (200 B.C.E.–70 C.E.), and an epitome of Roman history which proved that the successors to the Roman emperors were the Christian kings of Spain.

I believe that we can add geography to philosophy and history as part of the literary expression for consolation among the Jews. Benjamin's *Itinerary* expresses concern for the exile. It presents evidence for biblical antecedents to contemporary phenomena. Finally, the *Itinerary* presents a symmetry of Jewish and non-Jewish sovereigns which would indicate that one ought to view Jewish life in Spain within a global context. Jews were not subjugated everywhere. They lived favorably with many peoples, including some fierce tribes. They entered into alliances and waged wars. Jews were successful traders who travelled to the uttermost parts of the world.

A reading of the Hebrew of the *Itinerary* indicates the presence of the bible. Biblical verses indicate the tranquility of the wise inhabitants of Constantinople who "sit every man under his vine and fig tree." The glory of the Head of the Exile is seen as the fulfillment of the prophecy that sovereignty was present in Israel. Nearly every place in Palestine, Syria, and Iraq is identified with its biblical antecedent. These biblical images become particularly prominent in Iraq and Persia where Benjamin identifies synagogues founded by Ezra and Daniel. The Jewish biblical presence remains in Egypt, where the storehouses built by Joseph survived. Each of these biblical figures would resonate in the minds of medieval Jews as part of a consolatory message. Ezra, Daniel, and Joseph had all served Israel in the time of its exile. Their continuing presence held forth continuing hope that God would send other deliverers to help His people.

Benjamin presents the world-wide concern for Israel in exile by his description of pious and ascetic Jews: Rabbi Asher was a pious recluse who ate no meat, and studied day and night; The Mourners of Zion ate no meat, wore black garments, and fasted daily except for the Sabbath and festivals; They lived in caves or underground houses. In the midst of prosperous communities the attempt to end the exile of Israel by lives of constant prayer and study might offer a message of consolation. Jews prayed at the Western Wall of the Temple, or carved their names on Rachel's grave or brought the bones of their ancestors to the tomb of Abraham as part of their pilgrimage. Continuity of religious tradition within the midst of change and upheaval provided a firm framework for the medieval Jew.

By reading the *Itinerary* Spanish Jews could find similarities with their coreligionists in other parts of the world. Benjamin creates a portrait of world Jewry which reveals Jews as participants in the highest circles of power and influence in many of the lands. The Pope had a Jewish bailiff; In Syria a Jew served as the astronomer to King Nur-ed-Din; The "Prince of Princes" in Cairo had a seat in the royal palace.

The lengthy description of the caliph in Baghdad is the most clear indication of Benjamin's consolatory message. The caliph is presented as possessing great benevolence toward Jews. He knew Hebrew and Jewish law. The hospitals and sanitarium of the caliph are examples that agree with the highest ideals of Judaism.

Benjamin parallels his portrait of the caliph in his description of the Head of the Exile. The Head of the Exile is borne through the streets with great pomp, venerated equally by Jew and Moslem. He sits with the Moslem princes, fulfilling the prophecy about Judah in Genesis 49:10. Benjamin's utilization of this verse is a key to his message of consolation. Jews, Christians, and Moslems had argued over the meaning of this biblical verse. Both Christianity and Islam insisted that since the Jews had no king, the scepter had passed from them. However, the exegetical literature of the Jews had argued that the descendant of King David who lived in Babylonia held sovereignty over the Jews.

Benjamin describes the money which came to the Exilarch from all over the Islamic world. With this money and the monies from his properties the Head of the Exile owned hospices, gardens, and plantations in Babylon.

The political configuration in Iraq during the latter half of the twelfth century precluded the glorious portrait that Benjamin wrote about both the caliph and the Head of the Exile. Benjamin was describing an idealized form of reality which reflected his message of consolation. Even if the power of the Exilarch was circumscribed because the caliph had lost territory, the office was still highly regarded by Jews in Islamic territory.

Spanish Jews could look back on the glory of Samuel Ibn Nagrella and his armies. Benjamin's survey of other Jewish communities indicated that military power remained a part of Jewish life. Jews received favorable treatment by Wallachians, Druses, and Mulahids. These tribes lived by plunder, but traded with Jews. In Tadmor and Khaibar Jews join with Moslems to fight against Christians. There were Jewish communities in India, which lived in the mountains, and waged war against Christians. Christians were not exclusively the opponents of Jewish armies. When they felt threatened, the Jewish community allied with Turks and Mongols to fight against the Persians. Benjamin revealed that Jews, like any contemporary nation, could wage wars and sustain military alliances. The ability to conquer and hold territory had been part of the biblical heritage of the Jewish people.

The *Itinerary* forms a network of consolation by its formulaic presentations. In Europe each community is listed with its governing members. Descriptions of Jewish communities in the Byzantine and Islamic spheres of influence tend to emphasize physical monuments which derive from the past glory of the Jewish people and their relationship to the local ruling power. Benjamin evaluates several communities as "suffering under the yoke of the exile" or, as "not under the rule of the gentiles." An enumeration of the communities which are free of gentile rule would indicate that they outnumber the captive communities.

In the Moslem world there is common veneration of biblical figures. The Ezekiel Synagogue in Kaphri was the site of a Jewish gathering which was attended by Moslems "because they love Ezekiel." The king of Persia resolved a conflict within the Jewish communities of Susa in order to provide a proper tomb for the veneration of the sepulcher of Daniel.

The *Itinerary* descibes Christian respect for Jewish holy places in Palestine, such as the Temple Mount or the Tomb of the Patriarchs at Hebron. According to Benjamin only Jews were permitted to enter the subterranian catacombs where the patriarchs were buried. Christians had to be satisfied with the buildings above the ground. Only once in the entire narrative does Benjamin report that Christians desecrated Jewish graves. The overall impression, from reading the *Itinerary*, is one of veneration and respect for Jewish holy places by Moslems and Christians.

Benjamin's message of hope and consolation was not the promise of divine intervention and the messianic deliverance. It was a consolation derived from the broadest perspective on Jewish life. Some communities were under subjugation, others were free. Political conditions could change for the better. Many Jewish communities could wage wars. All Jews had some form of autonomous government which was respected by the gentile powers. Monuments of the Jewish past were venerated by Moslems and Christians. The reward of Benjamin's journey was to be found in the vigor of Jewish communities he discovered in Europe, Asia, and Africa.

A Cultural Tradition:
Benjamin and His Translators

THE EARLY printings in Hebrew of Benjamin probably reflect the diverse scientific and cultural interests of Sephardic and Italian Jewry in the sixteenth century. These humanistic interests were mirrored in the Christian world which adopted Benjamin as an important source of information about commerce in the Orient. The bibliography of A. Asher, which we reprint in this volume, describes the poor quality of many of the translations. Of equal interest is Asher's rather spirited defense of Benjamin's veracity against the charges that he falsified his reports.

A. Asher (1800–1853), a bibliophile, was Benjamin's first Jewish translator into English. He founded a publishing company in Berlin whose catalogues are still useful to contemporary scholars of Judaica. Three years before his translation of Benjamin appeared he published a "Bibliographical Essay on the Collections of Voyages and Travels."

Asher's two-volume translation of Benjamin's *Itinerary* represented a unique approach to the work. In the first volume he presented a vocalized Hebrew text and translation. The second volume consisted of lengthy notes on the text which were written by two distinguished Jewish scholars of German Jewry, Leopold Zunz and Furchtegott Lebrecht. Zunz had published a monograph on the contributions made by Jewish scholars to the field of geographic studies from the medieval period through the nineteenth century. Originally published in German, Asher translated the essay for the second volume of Benjamin's *Itinerary*. Lebrecht contributed an essay on the Abbasid Caliphate to the second volume of Asher's translation. The Asher volumes represent the best efforts of German-Jewish scholarship during the nineteenth century. Careful attention is given to the corroboration of each name in the *Itinerary* with all other references in contemporary medieval sources.

The translation which we reprint in this volume was done by Marcus Nathan Adler (1837–1911). Adler was the eldest son of Rabbi Nathan Marcus Adler, chief rabbi of Britain. Raised in an enlightened Orthodox Jewish household, Adler received his M.A. from University College in the University of London. He was a fellow of the Royal Statistical Society, and one of the founders of the London Mathematical Society. Marcus Adler was noted for his work on behalf of education in England. For many years he was the confidential secretary to the British philanthropist, Sir Moses Montefiore.

Marcus Nathan Adler evidenced an interest in exotic Jewish communities. In 1900 he published a work on Chinese Jews. By 1907 his new edition of the Hebrew text, together with translation and notes, appeared. The two works reflect erudition both in Judaica and general medieval studies.

The Adler translation is a significant advance over the Asher. Asher worked from a poorly preserved Hebrew text which was based on early printed editions. Benjamin's *Itinerary* has many unusual words and place names. Without a proper manuscript tradition, the translator was left to the mercy of the printer, who often did not understand the text in front of him. Adler discovered a manuscript in the British Museum which had been purchased through the firm of A. Asher. The British Museum manuscript was the earliest text, and represented the most clear preservation of the readings.

Adler was a faithful translator. His English may seem a bit stilted to the modern reader. At times we discern an apologetic motif in his translation of certain Hebrew words. Benjamin calls all non-Jewish places of worship *Bamoth* which literally means "Pagan altar." Adler often translates *Bamoth* as "Churches." The word "Pilgrim" in the Adler text is a translation of the Hebrew word "*To'im*." Readers of the Hebrew text of Benjamin would know that he was referring to Christians who were *To'im* or "those in error." Mohammed himself did not escape Benjamin's acerbic tongue. The Hebrew text refers to him as "*HaMeshug-gah*," which means, "the insane." Adler's footnote suggests that the Hebrew word conveys the sense of an Arabic word which means "the one possessed by God." Adler's notes are succinct and reflect broad learning. We have interspersed them throughout the text.

Both Adler and Asher explain their interest in Benjamin's journeys as a contribution to the development of the science of geography. Their presentations indicate that they were part of the great era of Jewish scholarship which sought to demonstrate the contribution of Jews to the larger world. The late nineteenth and early twentieth century was a time of optimism and explora-tion. European Jews were becoming part of the intellectual life of Western Europe. Part of that intellectual vitality was the growth of a body of knowledge about areas of the world beyond Europe. To present Benjamin of Tudela in a scientific translation was to indicate to both the Jewish and Christian world that Jews participated in the very first generations of Europeans to explore the East. Perhaps it was this role for Benjamin's *Itinerary* which was part of the spirited defense of the accuracy of his account.

In the eighty years since Adler's translation, studies of both European and Near Eastern Jewry have advanced. We now have the letters of merchant traders which were discovered in the attic of the Cairo Synagogue shortly before Adler published his translation. These letters corroborate and augment the portrait of the mid-twelfth century in the *Itinerary*. We no longer need to defend Benjamin's accuracy. Adler and Asher have brilliantly framed the limits of how accurate Benjamin could have been. He relied upon direct observation and upon the reports of merchants who became his informants.

The Itinerary of Benjamin of Tudela is a unique perception of the medieval Jewish experience. It appears to be a narration of a journey which describes the author's observations of people and places. But the journey took place through many levels of reality: physical, economic, and religious. As a scion of the Jews of al-Andalus, Benjamin's vision had been formed to integrate all of these realities and to penetrate beyond to the metaphysical reality of the Jewish people and their God. By carefully reading his narrative, Benjamin becomes our guide to this world.

I would like to take this occasion to thank Mr. Joseph Simon for his help and encouragement during this project. He has a deep sense of the aesthetic, a passion for accuracy and beauty, and a great *joie de vivre*.

MICHAEL A. SIGNER

ADLER INTRODUCTION

Islam in the Middle Ages

THE ITINERARY OF Benjamin of Tudela throws a flashlight upon one of the most interesting stages in the development of nations. The history of the civilized world from the downfall of the Roman Empire to the present day may be summarized as the struggle between Cross and Crescent. This struggle is characterized by a persistent ebb and flow. Mohammed in 622 A.D. transformed, as if by magic, a cluster of Bedouin tribes into a warlike people. An Arabian Empire was formed, which reached from the Ebro to the Indus. Its further advance was stemmed in the year 732, just a hundred years after Mohammed's death, by Charles Martel, in the seven days' battle of Tours.

The progress of the culture of the Arabs was as rapid as had been that of their arms. Great cities such as Cairo and Baghdad were built. Commerce and manufactures flourished. The Jews, who enjoyed protection under the benign rule of the Caliphs, transmitted to the Arabs the learning and science of the Greeks. Schools and universities arose in all parts of the Empire. The dark age of Christendom proved to be the golden age of literature for Jew and Arab.

By the eleventh century, however, the Arabs had lost much of their martial spirit. Islam might have lost its ascendancy in the East had not the warlike Seljuk Turks, coming from the highlands of Central Asia, possessed themselves of the countries which, in days of old, constituted the Persian Empire under Darius. The Seljuks became ready converts to Islam, and upheld the failing strength of the Arabs.

It was the ill-treatment by the Seljuks of the Christian pilgrims to Palestine which aroused Christian Europe and led to the First Crusade. The feudal system adopted by the Seljuks caused endless dissension among their petty sovereigns, called "Atabegs," all of whom were nominally vassals of the Caliph at Baghdad. Thus it came about that Islamism, divided against itself, offered but a poor resistance to the advance of the Christians. The Crusaders had little difficulty in making their way to Palestine. They captured Jerusalem, and established the Latin kingdom there.

By the middle of the twelfth century Mohammedan power had shrunk to smaller dimensions. Not only did the Franks hold Palestine and all the important posts on the Syrian coast, but, by the capture of Lesser Armenia, Antioch, and Edessa, they had driven a wedge into Syria, and extended their conquests even beyond the Euphrates.

At length there came a pause in the decline of Islam, Zengi, a powerful Seljuk Atabeg, in 1144 captured Edessa, the outpost of Christendom; and the Second Crusade, led by the Emperor Conrad of Germany and by King Louis VII of France, failed to effect the recapture of the fortress. Nureddin, the far-sighted son and successor of Zengi, and later on Saladin, a Kurd, trained at his court, discovered how to restore the fallen might of Islam and expel the Franks from Asia. A necessary preliminary step was to put an end to the dissensions of the Atabeg rulers. Nureddin did this effectually by himself annexing their dominions. His next step was to gain possession of Egypt, and thereby isolate the Latin Kingdom. Genoa, Pisa, and Venice, the three Italian republics who among them had command of the sea, were too selfish and too intent upon their commercial interests to interfere with the designs of the Saracens. The Latin king Amalric had for some years sought to gain a foothold in Egypt. In November, 1168, he led the Christian army as far as the Nile, and was about to seize Fostat, the old unfortified Arab metropolis of Egypt. The inhabitants, however, preferred to set fire to the city rather than that it should fall into the hands of the Christians. To this very day many traces may be seen in the neighborhood of Cairo of this conflagration. Nureddin's army, in which Saladin held a subordinate command, by a timely arrival on the scene forced the Franks to retreat, and the Saracens were acclaimed as deliverers.

The nominal ruler of Egypt at that time was El-Adid, the Fatimite Caliph, and he made Saladin his Vizier, little thinking that that modest officer would soon supplant him. So efficiently did Saladin administer the country that in a few months it had regained its prosperity, despite the five years of devastating war which had preceded.

At this juncture the traveller Rabbi Benjamin came to Egypt. Some three years earlier he had left his native place—Tudela, on the Ebro, in the north of Spain. After passing through the prosperous towns which lie on the Gulf of Lyons, he visited Rome and South Italy. From Otranto he crossed over to Corfu, traversed Greece, and then came to Constantinople, of which he gives an interesting account. Very telling, for example, are the words: "They hire from amongst all nations warriors called Barbarians to fight with the Sultan of the Seljuks; for the natives are not warlike, but are as women who have no strength to fight." After visiting the Islands of the Aegean, as well as Rhodes and Cyprus, he passed on to Antioch, and followed the well-known southern route skirting the Mediterranean, visiting the important cities along the coast, all of which were then in the hands of the Franks.

Having regard to the strained relations between the Christians and Saracens, and to the fights and forays of the Latin knights, we can understand that Benjamin had to follow a very circuitous way to enable him to visit all the places of note in Palestine. From Damascus, which was then the capital of Nureddin's empire, he travelled along with safety until he reached Baghdad, the city of the Caliph, of whom he has much to tell.

It is unlikely that he went far into Persia, which at that time was in a chaotic state, and where the Jews were much oppressed. From Basra, at the mouth of the Tigris, he probably visited the island of Kish in the Persian Gulf, which in the Middle Ages was a great emporium of commerce, and thence proceeded to Egypt by way of Aden and Assuan.

Benjamin gives us a vivid sketch of the Egypt of his day. Peace and plenty seemed to prevail in the country. This happy state of things was entirely due to the wise measures taken by Saladin who, however, kept himself so studiously in the background that not even his name is mentioned in the Itinerary. The deposition of the Fatimite Caliph on Friday, September 10, 1171, and his subsequent death, caused little stir. Saladin continued to govern Egypt as Nureddin's lieutenant. In due course he made himself master of Barca and Tripoli; then he conquered Arabia Felix and the Sudan, and after Nureddin's death he had no difficulty in annexing his old master's dominions. The Christian nations viewed his rapidly growing power with natural alarm.

About that time news had reached Europe that a powerful Christian king named Prester John, who reigned over a people coming from Central Asia, had invaded Western Asia and inflicted a crushing defeat upon a Moslem army. Pope Alexander III conceived the hope that a useful ally could be found in this priest-king, who would support and uphold the Christian dominion in Asia. He accordingly dispatched his physician, Philip, on a mission to this mysterious potentate to secure his help against the Mohammedans. The envoy never returned.

Benjamin is one of the very few writers of the Middle Ages who gives us an account of these subjects of Prester John. They were no other than the infidels, the sons of Ghuz, or Kofar-al-Turak, the wild flat-nosed Mongol hordes from the Tartary Steppes who, in Benjamin's quaint language, "worship the wind and live in the wilderness, who eat no bread and drink no wine, but feed on uncooked meat. They have no noses—in lieu thereof they have two small holes through which they breathe."

These were not men likely to help the Christians. On the contrary, as is so fully described in Benjamin's Itinerary, they broke the power of Sultan Sinjar, the mighty Shah of Persia who, had he been spared by the men of Ghuz, would have proved a serious menace to Saladin.

It took Saladin some years to consolidate his empire. In 1187 he felt himself in a position to engage the Franks in a decisive conflict. At the battle of Tiberias, Guy, the Latin king, was defeated and taken prisoner. The Knights-Templars and Hospitalers, of whose doings at Jerusalem Benjamin gives us particulars, either shared the fate of the king or were slain in action. Jerusalem fell soon afterwards. Pope Alexander III roused the conscience of Europe, and induced the pick of chivalry to embark upon the Third Crusade in 1189. But the prowess of the Emperor Frederic Barbarossa, the gallantry of Richard I of England, the astuteness of Philip Augustus of France, were of no avail. The Fourth and Fifth Crusades were equally unsuccessful, and the tide of Islam's success rose high.

After Saladin's death his empire gradually crumbled to pieces, and under Ghenghis Khan an invasion took place of hordes of Mongols and Tartars, of whom the Ghuz had been merely the precursors. They overran China and Russia, Persia, and parts of Western Asia. The effete Caliphate at Baghdad was overthrown, but to Islam itself fresh life was imparted. The rapid decline of the Mongol power at the end of the thirteenth century gave free scope to the rise of the Ottoman Turks, who had been driven from their haunts east of the Caspian Sea. Like their kinsmen, the Seljuks, they settled in Asia Minor, and embraced the Mohammedan faith, an example which many Mongols followed. The converts proved trusty warriors to fight the cause of Islam, which gradually attained the zenith of success. On May 29, 1453, Constantinople was captured by the Turks, and an end was made of the Byzantine Empire. Eastern Europe was subsequently overrun by them, and it was not until John Sobieski defeated the Turks under the walls of Vienna in 1683 that their victorious career was checked.

Then at last the tide of Islam turned, and its fortunes have been ebbing ever since. At the present day little territory remains to them in Europe. India and Egypt are now subject to England; Russia has annexed Central Asia; France rules Algiers and Tunis. One wonders whether there will be a pause in this steady decline of Islam, and whether the prophetic words of Scripture will continue to hold good: "He will be a wild man, his hand will be against every man, and every man's hand against him, and he shall dwell in the presence of all his brethren."

This brief consideration of the struggle between Cross and Crescent may serve to indicate the importance of the revival of Islam, which took place between the Second and Third Crusades, at the time when Benjamin wrote his Itinerary.

The Object of Benjamin's Journey

WE MAY ASK what induced Benjamin to undertake his travels? What object or mission was he carrying out?

It must be explained that the Jew in the Middle Ages was much given to travel. He was the Wandering Jew, who kept up communications between one country and another. He had a natural aptitude for trade and travel. His people were scattered to the four corners of the earth. As we can see from Benjamin's Itinerary, there was scarcely a city of importance where Jews could not be found. In the sacred tongue they possessed a common language, and wherever they went they could rely upon a hospitable reception from their co-religionists. Travelling was, therefore, to them comparatively easy, and the bond of common interest always supplied a motive. Like Joseph, the traveller would be dispatched with the injunction: "I pray thee see whether it be well with thy brethren, and bring me word again."

If this was the case in times when toleration and protection were extended to the Jews, how much stronger must have grown the desire for intercommunication at the time of the Crusades. The most prosperous communities in Germany, and the Jewish congregations that lay along the route to Palestine, had been exterminated or dispersed, and even in Spain, where the Jews had enjoyed complete security for centuries, they were being pitilessly persecuted in the Moorish kingdom of Cordova.

It is not unlikely, therefore, that Benjamin may have undertaken his journey with the object of finding out where his expatriated brethren might find an asylum. It will be noted that Benjamin seems to use every effort to trace and to afford particulars of independent communities of Jews, who had chiefs of their own, and owed no allegiance to the foreigner.

He may have had trade and mercantile operations in view. He certainly dwells on matters of commercial interest with considerable detail. Probably he was actuated by both motives, coupled with the pious wish of making a pilgrimage to the land of his fathers.

Whatever his intentions may have been, we owe Benjamin no small debt of gratitude for handing to posterity records that form a unique contribution to our knowledge of geography and ethnology in the Middle Ages.

Bibliography

THE ITINERARY OF Rabbi Benjamin of Tudela, prepared and published by A. Asher, is the best edition of the diary of that traveller. The first volume appeared in 1840, and contained a carefully compiled Hebrew text with vowel points, together with an English translation and a bibliographical account. A second volume appeared in 1841 containing elaborate notes by Asher himself and by such eminent scholars as Zunz and Rapoport, together with a valuable essay by the former on the Geographical Literature of the Jews, and on the Geography of Palestine, also an Essay by Lebrecht on the Caliphate of Baghdad.

In addition to twenty-three separate reprints and translations enumerated by Asher, various others have since appeared from time to time, but all of them are based upon the two editions of the text from which he compiled his work. These were the Editio Princeps, printed by Eliezer ben Gershon at Constantinople in 1543, and the Ferrara Edition of 1556, printed by Abraham Usque, the editor of the famous "Jews" Bible in Spanish.

Asher himself more than once deplores the fact that he had not a single MS. to resort to when confronted by doubtful or divergent readings in the texts before him. I have, however, been fortunate enough to be able to trace and examine three complete MSS. of Benjamin's Travels, as well as large fragments belonging to two other MSS., and these I have embodied in my present collation. The following is a brief description of the MSS.:

1. BM, a MS. in the British Museum. It is bound up with some of Maimonides' works, several Midrashic tracts, a commentary on the Hagadah by Joseph Gikatilia, and an extract from Abarbanel's commentary on Isaiah; it forms part of the Almanzi col-

lection, which curiously enough was purchased by the British Museum from Asher & Co. in October, 1865, some twenty years after Asher's death.

This MS. is the groundwork of the text I have adopted.

2. R, or the Roman MS., in the Casanatense library at Rome.

3. E, a MS. now in the possession of Herr Epstein of Vienna, who acquired it from Halberstamm's collection. The only reliable clue as to the date of this MS. is the license of the censor: "visto per me fra Luigi da Bologna Juglio 1599."

4. O, in the Oppenheim collection of the Bodleian Library.

5. B, also in the Oppenheim collection of the Bodleian Library.

In addition to the critical text, I give a translation of the British Museum MS., and add brief notes thereto. I have purposely confined the latter to small dimensions in view of the fact that Asher's notes, the Jewish Encyclopaedia, and the works of such writers as Graetz and others, will enable the reader to acquire further information on the various incidents, personages, and places referred to by Benjamin. I would, however, especially mention a work by Mr. C. Raymond Beazley entitled "The Dawn of Modern Geography," particularly his second volume, published in 1901. The frank and friendly manner in which the writer does justice to the merits of the Jewish traveller contrasts favorably with the petty and malignant comments of certain non-Jewish commentators, of which Asher repeatedly complains.

MARCUS N. ADLER
May 27, 1907

ASHER INTRODUCTION

VERY STUDENT must have felt, with myself, the entire want of a work on the Geography of the Middle Ages. Whilst on one hand Herodotus, Strabo, and the other ancient geographers have found editors and annotators without number, and on the other, not only individuals but societies have labored to make us acquainted with the present state of the world, comparatively nothing has been done to throw light on that portion of geography which comprises the ages called the dark. Thus, the curious in geography have abundant means of becoming acquainted with the political state of our planet in the times of Alexander and of Augustus, of Charles V and Victoria, but are at an utter loss for a work which treats the same subject at the period of the Crusades. Although these remarkable wars have found able historians —geography, the sister science, or rather the hand maiden of history, has been neglected to an astonishing degree. To remedy this neglect and furnish materials for a geography of the Middle Ages, is the aim of the present work, and the *Itinerary of R. Benjamin of Tudela* has been selected for that purpose; not only because it contains more facts and fewer fables than any other contemporary production which has come down to us, but also because it describes a very large portion of the earth known in the twelfth century.

I am fully aware that what I now offer to the public are but scanty contributions towards the science, the study of which I aim to promote, but I hope to continue these labors to make this work a book of reference to the student of Middle Ages and comparative geography. The materials will be furnished by comparing unedited contemporary authors, both European and Oriental, as well as by unremitting attention to those accounts which may be published by travellers of all nations. I hope that the distribution of copies of this work, which has been kindly promised by the London and Paris Royal Geographical Societies, will tend to promote my humble endeavours: a few more travellers like Major Rawlinson and a great portion of my aim will be accomplished.

I consider it necessary to state, that the striking similarity of this Itinerary to that of Marco Polo, has induced me to avail myself as much as possible of the plan and the researches of Mr. Marsden, the able editor of the former; and I shall feel proud if I succeed in establishing the title of a good imitator.

The author, Rabbi Benjamin Ben Jonah of Tudela, a Jewish merchant, began his travels about 1160 and his itinerary comprises a great portion of the then known world.

The only authority, which we can quote respecting the name of this traveller, is the preface to this Itinerary, the authenticity of which, though evidently by a later hand, we have no reason to doubt.

That Benjamin was a Jew, is too evident to require any further proof, and if we examine his work with any degree of attention, and compare it with similar productions, we shall be forced to admit, that he could only have been a merchant, who would be induced to notice, with so much accuracy, the state of trade in the towns and countries he visited. A glance at the article "commerce" of our index will be found strongly to corroborate the assertion that commerce was the vocation of our traveller.

The double object of his travels thus becomes evident: like many other Mohammedan and Christian pilgrims of the Middle Ages, Rabbi Benjamin visited Jerusalem, the city, and Baghdad, the seat of the last princes of his nation, and availed himself of this pilgrimage to collect such information as might be agreeable and useful to his brethren. He was aware of their attachment to those sites and monuments, which attest their former grandeur and to which they still look up with sweet melancholy. He felt the existence of that magic, invisible tie, which even in our days of indifferentism, roused the sympathy of all European Israelites in favor of the oppressed at Damascus, but he also knew, that commerce was almost their only means of support and its success the surest way to gain influence with the princes whose yoke oppressed the Jews of his own, and alas! of many succeeding ages. These considerations gave the book its present form; the accounts of the state of the Jews in the countries he saw or heard of, are ever varied by excellent notices and business-like remarks upon the trade carried on in the cities he describes, and the Itinerary claims, in as high a degree, the attention of the historian, as it does that of the theologian.

His visit to Rome must have taken place subsequent to 1159; that he was at Constantinople probably in December 1161; and that his account of Egypt, which almost concludes the work, must have been written prior to 1171. If we add to these dates, which have been obtained by an examination of the text, that of his return, as given in the preface, we shall find that the narrative refers to a period of about fourteen years, viz. from 1159 or 60, to 1173.

One very peculiar feature of this work, by which its contents are divided into "what he saw" and "what he heard," as the preface has it, requires particular notice.

In many towns on the route from Saragossa to Baghdad, Rabbi Benjamin mentions the names of the principal Jews, Elders, and Wardens of the congregations he met with. That a great number

of the persons enumerated by R. Benjamin really were his con-
temporaries, and the particulars he incidentally mentions of them,
are corroborated by other authorities. We therefore do not
hesitate to assert, that R. Benjamin visited all those towns of
which he names the Elders and principals, and that the first portion of his narrative comprises an account of "what he saw."

But with the very first stage beyond Baghdad, all such notices
cease, and except those of two Princes and of two Rabbis, we look
in vain for any other names. So very remarkable a difference between this and the preceding part of the work, leads us to assert,
that R. Benjamin's travels did not extend beyond Baghdad, and
that he there wrote down the second portion of our work, consisting of "what he heard." Baghdad, at this time, the seat of the
Prince of the captivity, must have attracted numerous Jewish
pilgrims from all regions, and beyond doubt was the fittest place
for gathering those notices of the Jews, and of trade in different
parts of the world, the collecting of which was the aim of R.
Benjamin's labors.

The languages in which Rabbi Benjamin's Itinerary is composed, is that which has been called Rabbinic Hebrew, an idiom
in which a great many of the words of scriptural origin have entirely changed their primitive import, and which has been enriched by many other terms of comparatively modern date.

The style of our narrative proves that its author was without
any pretensions to learning; it is the account of a very plain Jewish
merchant, who probably preferred the idiom in which he wrote,
because he understood still less of any other. The most learned
of his translators have been puzzled by the language and the style.

The history of this Itinerary is remarkable in many respects.
It appears early to have gained much credit among Jews and Chris-

tians, and the multiplied editions of it prove that it has always been in request among the learned. Its general veracity was acknowledged by the numerous quotations from, and references to, its contents, and until within a comparatively recent period, nobody doubted the authenticity of the travels. But these favorable views underwent a change in the seventeenth and eighteenth centuries: Theologians saw in R. Benjamin's reports nothing but an attempt to aggrandize the real number, and to represent under bland colors, the state of the Jews in remote countries. Although eminent historians admitted, and quoted Rabbi Benjamin's authority, they attempted to prove that these travels had never been performed, but were the compilations of an ignorant Jew, who had perhaps never left Tudela.

We might claim in refutation of the ill-supported doubts of these authors, the high and undeniable authority of Rapaport, Zunz, and Tafel, and the labors of Mr. Lebrecht, who not only consider the work authentic, but have in their notes vindicated R. Benjamin against his accusers. Yet, it may with truth be insisted, that the least equivocal proofs of its being an honest, however incomplete, account of what he actually saw or learned on the spot, are to be drawn from the relation itself. There numerous instances will present themselves of minute peculiarities and of incidental notices, geographical, historical, and biographical, reported by him and confirmed by the testimony of other ancient and modern authors and travellers, which he could neither have invented nor borrowed from others. Certainly it is the evidence of these coincidences, rather than any force of argument, that is likely to produce conviction in the minds of those, who are unwilling to be thought credulous. This vindication, generally, is not founded upon arguments, but upon an impartial examination of the particular details, which having been compared with and brought to the test of modern and contemporary observation, will be found remarkably correct.

The information contained in this work, and upon the merits of which it claims the attention of the learned, may be comprised under the following heads:

a. R. Benjamin's narrative contains the fullest account extant of the state and number of the Jews in the twelfth century.

b. It furnishes the best materials for the history of the commerce of Europe, Asia, and Africa at the time of the Crusades.

c. Our author is the first European, who notices with accuracy the sect of the Assassins in Syria and Persia, the trade with India (of the produce of which the Island of Kish was the principal emporium), and who distinctly mentions China and describes the dangers attendant upon a navigation of the ocean, which intervenes between that country and Ceylon.

d. The whole work abounds in interesting, correct, and authentic information on the state of the three quarters of the globe known at his time and in consideration of these advantages, stands without a rival in the literary history of the Middle Ages. None of the productions of this period are as free from fables and superstitions as the Itinerary of Rabbi Benjamin of Tudela.

An attentive study of the narrative in its present state, however, has forced upon us the conviction that what we possess, is but an abridgement of the original journal, which in this respect, and in many others, shared the fate of Pethachia's and Marco Polo's works.

It will further be observed that the descriptions of ten cities, and the two episodes contained in the work (a. Rome, Constantinople, Nablous, Jerusalem, Damascus, Baghdad, Thema, Chulam, Cairo, and Alexandria; and b. The history of El-Roy and the expedition against the Ghuz.) take up, in extent, more than one half of the whole, whereas about two hundred cities, some of which must have been of tantamount interest in many points of view, are noticed so briefly, that all the information concerning them is disposed of in a very narrow space; nor is it likely, that Rabbi Benjamin should have passed over in silence the commercial relations of Germany, where he mentions the city of Ratisbon and other towns, which at his time absorbed most of the trade of that country.

But these omissions are not the only disadvantage which we have to deplore, another formidable inconvenience arose from the ignorance of those transcribers, from whose copies the first editions were printed. By their misconceptions our author is often obscured, whilst their inaccuracies of orthography render it, in many instances, a matter of the utmost difficulty to recognize the proper names of persons and places. The letters of the idiom in which R. Benjamin wrote, are not fit to express with accuracy, French, Italian, Greek, and Arabic appellations; and as the text was written, of course, without the Hebrew vowel points, mistakes were not easily avoided.

Well aware of all these disadvantages, we have spared no labor nor expense in our attempts to discover a complete, ancient, and genuine manuscript. But neither in Europe nor in Egypt, have we been able to discover this desideratum. Our labor in this respect has been confined, necessarily, to comparing the two first, original editions, the second of which had not been consulted by any former editor or translator. We have also added the vowel points, by which the work becomes by far more intelligible to the general reader, and we hope not to be taxed with presumption if we assert, that our text, faulty as it must necessarily be, is still superior to any hitherto published.

A. ASHER
Berlin, December 1840

HEBREW INTRODUCTION

THIS IS the book of travels, which was compiled by Rabbi Benjamin, the son of Jonah, of the land of Navarre—his repose be in Paradise. The said Rabbi Benjamin set forth from Tudela, his native city, and passed through many remote countries, as is related in his book. In every place which he entered, he made a record of all that he saw, or was told of by trustworthy persons—matters not previously heard of in the land of Sepharad [Spain]. Also he mentions some of the sages and illustrious men residing in each place. He brought this book with him on his return to the country of Castile, in the year 4933 (C.E. 1173). The said Rabbi Benjamin is a wise and understanding man, learned in the Law and the Halacha, and wherever we have tested his statements we have found them accurate, true to fact and consistent; for he is a trustworthy man.

There is a considerable difference of opinion as to the exact dates at which Benjamin began and completed his journey. In my opinion, the period can be placed within a very narrow compass. Early in his journey he visited Rome, where he found R. Jechiel to be the steward of the household of Pope Alexander. This can be no other than Pope Alexander III (1159–1181), who played so important a part in the struggle between King Henry II and Thomas a Becket. The German Emperor, Frederick Barbarossa, supported the anti-Pope Victor IV, and in consequence Alexander had to leave Rome soon after his election in 1159 and before his consecration. He did not return to settle down permanently in Rome until November 23, 1165, but was forced to leave again in 1167. Consequently Benjamin must have been in Rome between the end of 1165 and 1167. Benjamin terminated his travels by passing from Egypt to Sicily and Italy, then crossing the Alps and visiting Germany. In Cairo he found that the Fatimite Caliph was the acknowledged ruler. The Caliph here referred to must have been El-'Âdid, who died on Monday, September 13, 1171—being the last of the Fatimite line. A short time before his death, Saladin had become the virtual ruler of Egypt, and had ordered the Khotba to be read in the name of the Abbaside Caliph el-Mostadi of Baghdad. It is clear, therefore, that Benjamin's absence from Europe must be placed between the years 1166 and 1171. Benjamin on his return journey passed through Sicily when the island was no longer governed by a viceroy. King William II (the Good) attained his majority in 1169, and Benjamin's visit took place subsequently. It will be found in the course of the narrative that not a single statement by Benjamin is inconsistent with this determination of date. [Adler]

The Itinerary of Benjamin of Tudela

HIS BOOK COMMENCES AS FOLLOWS

Europe

I JOURNEYED first from my native town to the city of Saragos- *Saragossa*
sa, and thence by way of the River Ebro to Tortosa. From *Tortosa*
there I went a journey of two days to the ancient city of Tar- *Tarragona*
ragona with its Cyclopean and Greek buildings. The like *Barcelona*
thereof is not found among any of the buildings in the country of Sepharad. It is situated by the sea, and two days' journey
from the city of Barcelona, where there is a holy congregation,
including sages, wise and illustrious men, such as R. Shesheth,
R. Shealtiel, R. Solomon, and R. Abraham, son of Chisdai.

> Here and generally in this narrative the letter R is used as an abbrevia-
> tion for Rabbi. It must be inferred from the context here, as well
> as from other passages, that when Benjamin mentions the number
> of Jews residing at a particular place he refers to the heads of families.
> [Adler]

This is a small and beautiful city, lying upon the seacoast. Merchants come thither from all quarters with their wares: from
Greece, from Pisa, Genoa, Sicily, Alexandria in Egypt, Palestine,
Africa and all its coasts. Thence it is a day and a half to Gerona, *Gerona*
in which there is a small congregation of Jews.

A three days' journey takes one to Narbonne, which is a city *Narbonne*
pre-eminent for learning; thence the Torah (Law) goes forth to
all countries. Sages, and great and illustrious men abide here. At
their head is R. Kalonymos, the son of the great and illustrious
R. Todros of the seed of David, whose pedigree is established. He
possesses hereditaments and lands given him by the ruler of the
city, of which no man can forcibly dispossess him. Prominent in

the community is R. Abraham, head of the Academy: also R. Machir and R. Judah, and many other distinguished scholars. At the present day 300 Jews are there.

Beziers   Thence it is four parasangs to the city of Beziers, where there
Montpellier is a congregation of learned men. At their head is R. Solomon Chalafta, R. Joseph, and R. Nethanel. Thence it is two days to Har Gaash which is called Montpellier. This is a place well situated for commerce. It is about a parasang from the sea, and men come for business there from all quarters, from Edom, Ishmael, the land Algarve, Lombardy, the dominion of Rome the Great, from all the land of Egypt, Palestine, Greece, France, Asia, and England. People of all nations are found there doing business through the medium of the Genoese and Pisans. In the city there are scholars of great eminence, at their head being R. Reuben, son of Todros, R. Nathan, son of Zechariah, and R. Samuel, their chief rabbi, also R. Solomon and R. Mordecai. They have among them houses of learning devoted to the study of the Talmud. Among the community are men both rich and charitable, who lend a helping hand to all that come to them.

Lunel   From Montpellier it is four parasangs to Lunel, in which there is a congregation of Israelites, who study the Law day and night. Here lived Rabbenu Meshullam the great rabbi, since deceased, and his five sons, who are wise, great and wealthy, namely: R. Joseph, R. Jacob, R. Aaron, and R. Asher, the recluse, who dwells apart from the world; he pores over his books day and night, fasts periodically and abstains from all meat. He is a great scholar of the Talmud. At Lunel live also their brother-in-law R. Moses, the chief rabbi, R. Samuel the elder, R. Ulsarnu, R. Solomon Hacohen, and R. Judah the Physician, the son of Tibbon, the Sephardi. The students that come from distant lands to learn the Law are taught, boarded, lodged and clothed by the congregation, so long as they attend the house of study. The community has wise, understanding and saintly men of great benevolence, who lend a helping hand to all their brethren both far and near. The congregation consists of about 300 Jews—may the Lord preserve them.

From there it is two parasangs to Posquières, which is a large *Posquières* place containing about 400 Jews, with an Academy under the auspices of the great Rabbi, R. Abraham, son of David, of blessed memory, an energetic and wise man, great as a talmudical authority. People come to him from a distance to learn the Law at his lips, and they find rest in his house, and he teaches them. Of those who are without means he also pays the expenses, for he is very rich. The munificent R. Joseph, son of Menachem, also dwells here, and R. Benveniste, R. Benjamin, R. Abraham and R. Isaac, son of R. Meir of blessed memory.

Thence it is four parasangs to the suburb Bourg de St. Gilles, in which place there are about a hundred Jews. Wise men abide there; at their head being R. Isaac, son of Jacob, R. Abraham, son of Judah, R. Eleazar, R. Jacob, R. Isaac, R. Moses and R. Jacob, son of rabbi Levi of blessed memory. This is a place of pilgrimage of the Gentiles who come hither from the ends of the earth. It is only three miles from the sea, and is situated upon the great River Rhone, which flows through the whole land of Provence. Here dwells the illustrious R. Abba Mari, son of the late R. Isaac; he is the bailiff of Count Raymond.

> The Abbey of St. Aegidius was much resorted to in the Middle Ages. The Jews of Beaucaire, and the neighbourhood, enjoyed the patronage of Raymond V, Count of Toulouse, called by the Troubadour poets "the good Duke." [Adler]

Thence it is three parasangs to the city of Arles, which has *Arles* about 200 Israelites, at their head being R. Moses, R. Tobias, R. Isaiah, R. Solomon, the chief rabbi R. Nathan, and R. Abba Mari, since deceased.

Marseilles From there it is three days' journey to Marseilles, which is a city of princely and wise citizens, possessing two congregations with about 300 Jews. One congregation dwells below on the shore by the sea, the other is in the castle above. They form a great academy of learned men, amongst them being R. Simeon, R. Solomon, R. Isaac, son of Abba Mari, R. Simeon, son of Antoli, and R. Jacob his brother; also R. Libero. These persons are at the head of the upper academy. At the head of the congregation below are R. Jacob Purpis, a wealthy man, and R. Abraham son of R. Meir, his son-in-law, and R. Isaac, son of the late R. Meir. It is a very busy city upon the seacoast.

Genoa From Marseilles one can take ship and in four days reach Genoa, which is also upon the sea. Here live two Jews, R. Samuel, son of Salim, and his brother, from the city of Ceuta, both of them good men. The city is surrounded by a wall, and the inhabitants are not governed by any king, but by judges whom they appoint at their pleasure. Each householder has a tower to his house, and at times of strife they fight from the tops of the towers with each other. They have command of the sea. They build ships which they call galleys, and make predatory attacks upon Edom and Ishmael and the land of Greece as far as Sicily, and they bring back to Genoa spoils from all these places. They are constantly at war with the men of Pisa. Between them and the Pisans there is a distance of two days' journey.

Pisa Pisa is a very great city, with about 10,000 turreted houses for battle at times of strife. All its inhabitants are mighty men. They possess neither king nor prince to govern them, but only the judges appointed by themselves. In this city are about twenty Jews, at their head being R. Moses, R. Chayim, and R. Joseph. The city is not surrounded by a wall. It is about six miles from the sea; the river which flows through the city provides it with ingress and egress for ships.

Lucca From Pisa it is four parasangs to the city of Lucca, which is the beginning of the frontier of Lombardy. In the city of Lucca are about forty Jews. It is a large place, and at the head of the Jews are R. David, R. Samuel, and R. Jacob.

Thence it is six days' journey to the great city of Rome. Rome is the head of the kingdoms of Christendom, and contains about 200 Jews, who occupy an honourable position and pay no tribute, and amongst them are officials of the Pope Alexander, the spiritual head of all Christendom. Great scholars reside here, at the head of them being R. Daniel, the chief rabbi, and R. Jechiel, an official of the Pope. He is a handsome young man of intelligence and wisdom, and he has the entry of the Pope's palace; for he is the steward of his house and of all that he has. He is a grandson of R. Nathan, who composed the Aruch and its commentaries. Other scholars are R. Joab, son of the chief rabbi R. Solomon, R. Menachem, head of the academy, R. Jechiel, who lives in Trastevere, and R. Benjamin, son of R. Shabbethai of blessed memory. Rome is divided into two parts by the River Tiber. In the one part is the great church which they call St. Peter's of Rome. The great Palace of Julius Caesar was also in Rome. There are many wonderful structures in the city, different from any others in the world. Including both its inhabited and ruined parts, Rome is about twenty-four miles in circumference. In the midst thereof there are eighty palaces belonging to eighty kings who lived there, each called Imperator, commencing from King Tarquinius down to Nero and Tiberius, who lived at the time of Jesus the Nazarene, ending with Pepin, who freed the land of Sepharad from Islam, and was father of Charlemagne.

There is a palace outside Rome (said to be of Titus). The Consul and his 300 Senators treated him with disfavour, because he failed to take Jerusalem till after three years, though they had bidden him to capture it within two.

In Rome is also the palace of Vespasianus, a great and very

strong building; also the Colosseum, in which edifice there are 365 sections, according to the days of the solar year; and the circumference of these palaces is three miles. There were battles fought here in olden times, and in the palace more than 100,000 men were slain, and there their bones remain piled up to the present day. The king caused to be engraved a representation of the battle and of the forces on either side facing one another, both warriors and horses, all in marble, to exhibit to the world the war of the days of old.

In Rome there is a cave which runs underground, and catacombs of King Tarmal Galsin and his royal consort who are to be found there, seated upon their thrones, and with them about a hundred royal personages. They are all embalmed and preserved to this day. In the church of St. John in the Lateran there are two bronze columns taken from the Temple, the handiwork of King Solomon, each column being engraved "Solomon the son of David." The Jews of Rome told me that every year upon the 9th of Ab [July-August] they found the columns exuding moisture like water. There also is the cave where Titus the son of Vespasianus stored the Temple vessels which he brought from Jerusalem. There is also a cave in a hill on one bank of the River Tiber where are the graves of the ten martyrs. In front of St. John in the Lateran there are statues of Samson in marble, with a spear in his hand, and of Absalom, the son of King David, and another of Constantinus the Great, who built Constantinople, and after whom it was called. The last-named statue is of bronze, the horse being overlaid with gold. Many other edifices are there, and remarkable sights beyond enumeration.

Capua   From Rome it is four days to Capua, the large town which King Capys built. It is a fine city, but its water is bad, and the country is fever-stricken. About 300 Jews live there, among them great scholars and esteemed persons, at their heads being R. Conso, his brother R. Israel, R. Zaken and the chief rabbi R. David, since deceased. They call this district the Principality.

From there one goes to Pozzuoli, which is called Sorrento the *Sorrento* Great, built by Zur, son of Hadadezer, when he fled in fear of David the king. The sea has risen and covered the city from its two sides, and at the present day one can still see the markets and towers which stood in the midst of the city.

> Professor Ray Lankester, in a lecture given on Dec. 29, 1903, at the Royal Institution, illustrated changes in the disposition of land and water by pointing to the identical ruined Temple referred to by Benjamin. It now stands high above the sea, and did so in the second and third centuries of the present era, but in the eighth and ninth centuries was so low, owing to the sinking of the land, that the lower parts of its marble pillars stood in the sea, and sea-shells grew in the crevices. [Adler]

A spring issues forth from beneath the ground containing the oil which is called petroleum. People collect it from the surface of the water and use it medicinally. There are also hot water springs to the number of about twenty, which issue from the ground and are situated near the sea, and every man who has any disease can go and bathe in them and get cured. All the afflicted of Lombardy visit it in the summertime for that purpose.

From this place a man can travel fifteen miles along a road under the mountains, a work executed by King Romulus who built the city of Rome. He was prompted to this by fear of King David and Joab his general. He built fortifications both upon the mountains and below the mountains reaching as far as the city of Naples.

Naples is a very strong city, lying upon the sea-board, and was *Naples* founded by the Greeks. About 500 Jews live here, amongst them R. Hezekiah, R. Shallum, R. Elijah Hacohen and R. Isaac of Har Napus, the chief rabbi of blessed memory.

Salerno Thence one proceeds by sea to the city of Salerno, where the Christians have a school of medicine. About 600 Jews dwell there. Among the scholars are R. Judah, son of R. Isaac, the son of Melchizedek, the great Rabbi, who came from the city of Siponto; also R. Solomon, R. Elijah the Greek, R. Abraham Narboni, and R. Hamon. It is a city with walls upon the land side, the other side bordering on the sea, and there is a very strong castle on the

Amalfi summit of the hill. Thence it is half a day's journey to Amalfi, where there are about twenty Jews, amongst them R. Hananel, the physician, R. Elisha, and Abu-al-gir, the prince. The inhabitants of the place are merchants engaged in trade, who do not sow or reap, because they dwell upon high hills and lofty crags, but buy everything for money. Nevertheless, they have an abundance of fruit, for it is a land of vineyards and olives, of gardens and plantations, and no one can go to war with them.

Benevento Thence it is a day's journey to Benevento, which is a city situated between the seacoast and a mountain, and possessing a community of about 200 Jews. At their head are R. Kalonymus, R. Zarach, and R. Abraham. From there it is two days' journey

Melfi/ to Melfi in the country of Apulia, which is the land of Pul, where
Apulia about 200 Jews reside, at their head being R. Achimaaz, R. Nathan, and R. Isaac. From Melfi it is about a day's journey

Ascoli to Ascoli, where there are about forty Jews, at their head being R. Consoli, R. Zemach, his son-in-law, and R. Joseph. From

Trani there it takes two days to Trani on the sea, where all the pilgrims gather to go to Jerusalem; for the port is a convenient one. A community of about 200 Israelites is there, at their head being R. Elijah, R. Nathan the Expounder, and R. Jacob. It is a great and beautiful city.

From there it is a day's journey to Colo di Bari, which is the great city which King William of Sicily destroyed. Neither Jews nor Gentiles live there at the present day in consequence of its destruction.

This city was destroyed by William the Bad in 1156. It was ordered to be restored by William the Good in 1169, so that Benjamin must have visited Bari before that date. We have here another clue as to the date of Benjamin's travels. [Adler]

Thence it is a day and a half to Taranto, which is under the government of Calabria, the inhabitants of which are Greek. It is a large city, and contains about 300 Jews, some of them men of learning, and at their head are R. Meir, R. Nathan, and R. Israel. *Taranto/ Calabria*

From Taranto it is a day's journey to Brindisi, which is on the seacoast. About ten Jews, who are dyers, reside here. It is two days' journey to Otranto, which is on the coast of the Greek sea. Here are about 500 Jews, at the head of them being R. Menachem, R. Caleb, R. Meir, and R. Mali. From Otranto it is a voyage of two days to Corfu, where only one Jew of the name of R. Joseph lives, and here ends the kingdom of Sicily. *Brindisi* *Otranto* *Corfu*

Thence it is two days' voyage to the land of Larta (Arta), which is the beginning of the dominions of Emanuel, Sovereign of the Greeks. It is a place containing about 100 Jews, at their head being R. Shelachiah and R. Hercules. From there it is two days to Aphilon (Achelous), a place in which reside about thirty Jews, at their head being R. Sabbattai. From there it takes half a day to Anatolica, which is situated on an arm of the sea. *Arta/Greece* *Achelous* *Anatolica*

From there it takes a day to Patras, which is the city which Antipater, King of the Greeks, built. He was one of the four successors of King Alexander. In the city there are several large old buildings, and about fifty Jews live here, at their head being R. Isaac, R. Jacob, and R. Samuel. Half a day's journey by way of the sea takes one to Kifto (Lepanto), where there are about 100 Jews, who live on the seacoast; at their head are R. Guri, R. Shallum, and R. Abraham. From there it is a journey of a day *Patras* *Lepanto* and a half to Crissa, where about 200 Jews live apart. They sow and reap on their own land; at their head are R. Solomon, R. Chayim, and R. Jedaiah. From there it is three days' journey

Corinth to the capital city of Corinth; here are about 300 Jews, at their head being R. Leon, R. Jacob, and R. Hezekiah.

Thebes Thence it is two days' journey to the great city of Thebes, where there are about 2,000 Jews. They are the most skilled artificers in silk and purple cloth throughout Greece. They have scholars learned in the Mishnah and the Talmud, and other prominent men, and at their head are the chief rabbi R. Kuti and his brother R. Moses, as well as R. Chiyah, R. Elijah Tirutot, and R. Joktan; and there are none like them in the land of the Greeks, except in the city of Constantinople. From Thebes it is a day's

Egripo journey to Egripo, which is a large city upon the seacoast, where merchants come from every quarter. About 200 Jews live there, at their head being R. Elijah Psalteri, R. Emanuel, and R. Caleb.

Jabustrisa From there it takes a day to Jabustrisa, which is a city upon the seacoast with about 100 Jews, at their head being R. Joseph, R. Elazar, R. Isaac, R. Samuel, and R. Nethaniah. From there it

Rabonica is a day's journey to Rabonica, where there are about 100 Jews.

From there it is a day's journey to Sinon Potamo, where there

Sinon Potamo/ are about fifty Jews, at their head being R. Solomon and R. Jacob.
Wallachia The city is situated at the foot of the hills of Wallachia. The nation called Wallachians live in those mountains. They are as swift as hinds, and they sweep down from the mountains to despoil and ravage the land of Greece. No man can go up and do battle against them, and no king can rule over them. They do not hold fast to the faith of the Nazarenes, but give themselves Jewish names. Some people say that they are Jews and, in fact, they call the Jews their brethren, and when they meet with them, though they rob them, they refrain from killing them as they kill the Greeks. They are altogether lawless.

Gardiki From there it is two days' journey to Gardiki, which is in ruins

and contains but a few Greeks and Jews. From there it is two
days' journey to Armylo, which is a large city on the sea, in- *Armylo*
habited by Venetians, Pisans, Genoese, and all the merchants who
come there; it is an extensive place, and contains about 400 Jews.
At their head are the chief rabbi R. Shiloh Lombardo, R. Joseph,
the warden, and R. Solomon, the leading man. Thence it is a day's
journey to Vissena, where there are about 100 Jews, at their head *Vissena*
being the chief rabbi R. Sabbattai, R. Solomon, and R. Jacob.

From there it is two days' voyage to the city of Salonica, built *Salonica*
by King Seleucus, one of the four successors who followed after
King Alexander. It is a very large city, with about 500 Jews, including the chief rabbi R. Samuel and his sons, who are scholars.
He is appointed by the king as head of the Jews. There is also
R. Sabbattai, his son-in-law, R. Elijah, and R. Michael. The Jews
are oppressed, and live by silk-weaving.

Thence it is two days' journey to Demetrizi, with about fifty *Demetrizi*
Jews. In this place live R. Isaiah, R. Machir, and R. Alib. Thence
it is two days to Drama, where there are about 140 Jews, at the *Drama*
head of them being R. Michael and R. Joseph. From there it is
one day's journey to Christopoli, where about twenty Jews live. *Christopoli*

A three days' voyage brings one to Abydos, which is upon an *Abydos*
arm of the sea which flows between the mountains, and after a
five days' journey the great city of Constantinople is reached. It *Constantinople*
is the capital of the whole land of Javan, which is called Greece.
Here is the residence of the King Emanuel the Emperor. Twelve
ministers are under him, each of whom has a palace in Constantinople and possesses castles and cities; they rule all the land. At
their head is the King Hipparchus, the second in command is the
Megas Domesticus, the third Dominus, the fourth is Megas
Ducas, and the fifth is Oeconomus Megalus—the others bear
names like these. The circumference of the city of Constantinople
is eighteen miles; half of it is surrounded by the sea, and half by

land, and it is situated upon two arms of the sea, one coming from the sea of Russia, and one from the sea of Sepharad.

All sorts of merchants come here from the land of Babylon, from the land of Shinar, from Persia, Media, and all the sovereignty of the land of Egypt, from the land of Canaan, and the empire of Russia, from Hungaria, Patzinakia, Khazaria, and the land of Lombardy and Sepharad.

> Patzinakia was the country from the Danube to the Dnieper, and corresponds with Dacia of classical times.
>
> The southern provinces of Russia were spoken of as the land of the Khazars, especially by Jewish writers, long after the Russian conquest about the year 1000, and the Crimea was known to European travellers as Gazaria. It took Rabbi Pethachia eight days to pass through the land of the Khazars. The ruling dynasty and most of the inhabitants embraced the Jewish religion. [Adler]

Constantinople is a busy city, and merchants come to it from every country by sea or land, and there is none like it in the world except Baghdad, the great city of Islam. In Constantinople is the church of Santa Sophia, and the seat of the Pope of the Greeks, since the Greeks do not obey the Pope of Rome. There are also churches according to the number of the days of the year. A quantity of wealth beyond telling is brought hither year by year as tribute from the two islands, and the castles and villages which are there. And the like of this wealth is not to be found in any other church in the world. And in this church there are pillars of gold and silver, and lamps of silver and gold more than a man can count. Close to the walls of the palace is also a place of amusement belonging to the king, which is called the Hippodrome, and every year on the anniversary of the birth of Jesus the king gives a great entertainment there. And in that place men from all the races of the world come before the king and queen with jugglery and without jugglery, and they introduce lions, leopards, bears, and wild asses, and they engage them in combat with one another; and the same thing is done with birds. No entertainment like this is to be found in any other land.

This King Emanuel built a great palace for the seat of his government upon the seacoast, in addition to the palaces which his fathers built, and he called its name Blachernae. He overlaid its columns and walls with gold and silver, and engraved thereon representations of the battles before his day and of his own combats. He also set up a throne of gold and of precious stones, and a golden crown was suspended by a gold chain over the throne, so arranged that he might sit thereunder. It was inlaid with jewels of priceless value, and at night time no lights were required, for every one could see by the light which the stones gave forth. Countless other buildings are to be met with in the city. From every part of the empire of Greece tribute is brought here every year, and they fill strongholds with garments of silk, purple, and gold. Like unto these storehouses and this wealth there is nothing in the whole world to be found. It is said that the tribute of the city amounts every year to 20,000 gold pieces, derived both from the rents of shops and markets, and from the tribute of merchants who enter by sea or land.

The Greek inhabitants are very rich in gold and precious stones, and they go clothed in garments of silk with gold embroidery, and they ride horses, and look like princes. Indeed, the land is very rich in all cloth stuffs, and in bread, meat, and wine.

Wealth like that of Constantinople is not to be found in the whole world. Here also are men learned in all the books of the Greeks, and they eat and drink, every man under his vine and his fig-tree.

They hire from amongst all nations warriors called Loazim (Barbarians) to fight with the Sultan Masud, King of the Togarmim (Seljuks), who are called Turks; for the natives are not warlike, but are as women who have no strength to fight.

No Jews live in the city, for they have been placed behind an inlet of the sea. An arm of the sea of Marmora shuts them in on the one side, and they are unable to go out except by way of the sea, when they want to do business with the inhabitants. In the Jewish quarter are about 2,000 Rabbanite Jews and about 500 Karaïtes, and a fence divides them. Amongst the scholars are several wise men, at their head being the chief rabbi R. Abtalion, R. Obadiah, R. Aaron Bechor Shoro, R. Joseph Shir-Guru, and R. Eliakim, the warden. And amongst them there are artificers in silk and many rich merchants. No Jew there is allowed to ride on horseback. The one exception is R. Solomon Hamitsri, who is the king's physician, and through whom the Jews enjoy considerable alleviation of their oppression. For their condition is very low, and there is much hatred against them, which is fostered by the tanners, who throw out their dirty water in the streets before the doors of the Jewish houses and defile the Jews' quarter. So the Greeks hate the Jews, good and bad alike, and subject them to great oppression, and beat them in the streets, and in every way treat them with rigour. Yet the Jews are rich and good, kindly and charitable, and bear their lot with cheerfulness. The district inhabited by the Jews is called Pera.

Rhaedestus From Constantinople it is two days' voyage to Rhaedestus, with a community of Israelites of about 400, at their head being R. Moses, R. Abijah, and R. Jacob. From there it is two days Gallipoli to Callipolis (Gallipoli), where there are about 200 Jews, at their head being R. Elijah Kapur, R. Shabbattai Zutro, and R. Isaac Megas, which means "great" in Greek. And from here it is two Kales days to Kales. Here there are about fifty Jews, at their head being R. Jacob and R. Judah. From here it is two days' journey to Mytilene the island of Mytilene, and there are Jewish congregations in ten localities on the island. Thence it is three days' voyage to the island Chios of Chios, where there are about 400 Jews, including R. Elijah

Heman and R. Shabtha. Here grow the trees from which mastic
is obtained. Two days' voyage takes one to the island of Samos,   *Samos*
where there are 300 Jews, at their head being R. Shemaria, R.
Obadiah, and R. Joel. The islands have many congregations of
Jews. From Samos it is three days to Rhodes, where there are   *Rhodes*
about 400 Jews, at their head being R. Abba, R. Hannanel, and
R. Elijah.

Europe to Asia

I T IS FOUR DAYS' VOYAGE from here to Cyprus, where   *Cyprus*
there are Rabbanite Jews and Karaïtes; there are also some
heretical Jews called Epikursin, whom the Israelites have
excommunicated in all places. They profane the eve of the
Sabbath, and observe the first night of the week, which is
the termination of the Sabbath.

> Ibn Ezra visited Cyprus before his arrival in London in 1158, when
> he wrote the *Sabbath Epistle*. It is not unlikely that the heterodox prac-
> tices of the sect of whom Benjamin here speaks had been put forward
> in certain books to which Ibn Ezra alludes, and induced him to com-
> pose the pamphlet in defence of the traditional mode of observance
> of the Sabbath day. [Adler]

From Cyprus it is four days' journey to Curicus (Kurch),   *Kurch/*
which is the beginning of the land called Armenia, and this is the   *Armenia*
frontier of the empire of Thoros, ruler of the mountains and king
of Armenia, whose dominions extend to the province of Trunia,
and to the country of the Togarmim or Turks. From there it is
two days' journey to Malmistras, which is Tarshish, situated by   *Malmistras*
the sea; and thus far extends the kingdom of the Javanim or
Greeks.

Thence it is two days' journey to Antioch the Great, situated   *Antioch/*
on the river Fur (Orontes), which is the river Jabbok, that flows   *Syria*
from Mount Lebanon and from the land of Hamath. This is the
great city which Antiochus the king built. The city lies by a lofty mountain, which is surrounded by the city wall. At the top
of the mountain is a well, from which a man appointed for that
purpose directs the water by means of twenty subterranean

passages to the houses of the great men of the city. The other part of the city is surrounded by the river. It is a strongly fortified city, and is under the sway of Prince Boemond Poitevin, surnamed le Baube. Ten Jews dwell here, engaged in glass-making, and at their head are R. Mordecai, R. Chayim, and R. Samuel. From *Ladikiya* here it is two days' journey to Lega, or Ladikiya, where there are about 100 Jews, at their head being R. Chayim and R. Joseph.

Gebela Thence it is two days' journey to Gebal (Gebela), which is Baal-Gad, at the foot of Lebanon. In the neighborhood dwells a people called Al-Hashishim. They do not believe in the religion of Islam, but follow one of their own folk, whom they regard as their prophet, and all that he tells them to do they carry out, whether for death or life. They call him the Sheik Al Hashishim, and he is known as their Elder. At his word these mountaineers go out and come in.

Hashishim—hemp-smokers—hence is derived the word "assassin." Ibn Batuta and other Arabic writers have much to say about the Assassins or Mulahids, as they call them. They are again referred to by Benjamin when he states that in Persia they haunted the mountainous district of Mulahid, under the sway of the Old Man of the Mountain. The manner in which the Sheik acquired influence over his followers is amusingly described by Marco Polo (*The Book of Ser Marco Polo*: translated and edited by Colonel Sir Henry Yule; London, 1903): "In a fertile and sequestered valley he placed every conceivable thing pleasant to man—luxurious palaces, delightful gardens, fair damsels skilled in music, dancing, and song, in short, a veritable paradise! When desirous of sending any of his band on some hazardous enterprise the Old Man would drug them and place them while unconscious in this glorious valley. But it was not for many days that they were allowed to revel in the joys of paradise. Another potion was given to them, and when the young men awoke they found themselves in the presence of the Old Man of the Mountain. In the hope of again possessing the joys of paradise they were ready to embark upon any desperate errand commanded by the Old Man." Marco

Polo mentions that the Old Man found crafty deputies, who with their followers settled in parts of Syria and Kurdistan. He adds that, in the year 1252, Alaü, lord of the Tartars of the Levant, made war against the Old Man, and slaughtered him with many of his followers. Yule gives a long list of murders or attempts at murder ascribed to the Assassins. Saladin's life was attempted in 1174–6. Prince Edward of England was slain at Acre in 1172. The sect is not quite extinct. They have spread to Bombay and Zanzibar, and number in Western India over 50,000. The mention of the Old Man of the Mountain will recall to the reader the story of Sinbad the Sailor in *The Arabian Nights*. [Adler]

Their principal seat is Kadmus, which is Kedemoth in the land of Sihon. They are faithful to each other, but a source of terror to their neighbors, killing even kings, at the cost of their own lives. The extent of their land is eight days' journey. And they are at war with the sons of Edom who are called the Franks, and with the ruler of Tripolis, which is Tarabulus el Sham. At Tripolis in years gone by there was an earthquake, when many Gentiles and Jews perished, for houses and walls fell upon them. There was great destruction at that time throughout the land of Israel, and more than 20,000 souls perished.

Thence it is a day's journey to the other Gebal (Gubail), which *Gubail* borders on the land of the children of Ammon, and here there are about 150 Jews. The place is under the rule of the Genoese, the name of the governor being Guillelmus Embriacus. Here was found a temple belonging to the children of Ammon in olden times, and an idol of theirs seated upon a throne or chair, and made of stone overlaid with gold. Two women are represented sitting, one on the right and one on the left of it, and there is an altar in front before which the Ammonites used to sacrifice and burn incense. There are about 200 Jews there, at their head being R. Meir, R. Jacob, and R. Simchah. The place is situated on the sea-border of the land of Israel.

Gubail, the ancient Gebal, was noted for its artificers and stonecutters. Cf. 1 Kings v. 32; Ezek. xxvii. 9. The Greeks named the place Byblos, the birthplace of Philo. The coins of Byblos have a representation of the Temple of Astarte. All along the coast we find remains of the worship of Baal Kronos and Baaltis, of Osiris and Isis, and it is probable that the worship of Adonis and Jupiter-Ammon led Benjamin to associate therewith the Ammonites. The reference to the children of Ammon is based on a misunderstanding, arising perhaps out of Ps. lxxxiii. 8. [Adler]

Beirut/
Lebanon

Sidon

From there it is two days' journey to Beirut, or Beeroth, where there are about fifty Jews, at their head being R. Solomon, R. Obadiah, and R. Joseph. Thence it is one day's journey to Saida, which is Sidon, a large city, with about twenty Jews. Ten miles therefrom a people dwell who are at war with the men of Sidon; they are called Druses, and are pagans of a lawless character. They inhabit the mountains and the clefts of the rocks; they have no king or ruler, but dwell independent in these high places, and their border extends to Mount Hermon, which is a three days' journey. They are steeped in vice, brothers marrying their sisters, and fathers their daughters. They have one feast-day in the year, when they all collect, both men and women, to eat and drink together, and they then interchange their wives. They say that at the time when the soul leaves the body it passes, in the case of a good man, into the body of a newborn child; and in the case of a bad man, into the body of a dog or an ass. Such are their foolish beliefs. There are no resident Jews among them, but a certain number of Jewish handicraftsmen and dyers come among them for the sake of trade, and then return, the people being favourable to the Jews. They roam over the mountains and hills, and no man can do battle with them.

The Quarterly Statements of the Palestine Exploration Fund for 1886 and 1889 give a good deal of information concerning the religion of the Druses. Their morality is there described as having been much maligned. [Adler]

From Sidon it is half a day's journey to Sarepta (Sarfend), which belongs to Sidon. Thence it is a half day to New Tyre (Sur), which Tyre
is a very fine city, with a harbour in its midst. At night-time those that levy dues throw iron chains from tower to tower, so that no man can go forth by boat or in any other way to rob the ships by night. There is no harbour like this in the whole world. Tyre is a beautiful city. It contains about 500 Jews, some of them scholars of the Talmud, at their head being R. Ephraim of Tyre, the Dayan, R. Meir from Carcassonne, and R. Abraham, head of the congregation. The Jews own sea-going vessels, and there are glass-makers amongst them who make that fine Tyrian glass-ware which is prized in all countries. In the vicinity is found sugar of a high class, for men plant it here, and people come from all lands to buy it. A man can ascend the walls of New Tyre and see ancient Tyre, which the sea has now covered, lying at a stone's throw from the new city. And should one care to go forth by boat, one can see the castles, market places, streets, and palaces, in the bed of the sea. New Tyre is a busy place of commerce, to which merchants flock from all quarters.

Tyre was noted for its glassware and sugar factories up to 1291, when it was abandoned by the Crusaders, and destroyed by the Moslems. [Adler]

One day's journey brings one to Acre, the Acco of old, which Acre
is on the borders of Asher; it is the commencement of the land of Israel. Situated by the Great Sea [Mediterranean], it possesses a large harbour for all the pilgrims who come to Jerusalem by ship. A stream runs in front of it, called the brook of Kedumim.

This name is applied to the Kishon, mentioned further on, celebrated in Deborah's song (Judg. v. 21), but it is about five miles south of Acre, the river nearest to the town being the Belus, noted for its fine sand suitable for glassmaking. It is not unlikely that R. Benjamin alludes to the celebrated ox-spring of which Arab writers have much to say. Mukkadasi writes in 985: "Outside the eastern city gate is a spring. This they call Ain al Bakar, relating how it was Adam—peace be upon him!—who discovered this spring, and gave his oxen water therefrom, whence its name." [Adler]

About 200 Jews live there, at their head being R. Zadok, R. Japheth, and R. Jonah. From there it is three parasangs to Haifa, which is Hahepher on the seaboard, and on the other side is Mount Carmel, at the foot of which there are many Jewish graves. On the mountain is the cave of Elijah, where the Christians have erected a structure call St. Elias. On the top of the mountain can be recognized the overthrown altar which Elijah repaired in the days of Ahab. The site of the altar is circular, about four cubits remain thereof, and at the foot of the mountain the brook Kishon flows. From here it is four parasangs to Capernaum, which is the village of Nahum, identical with Maon, the home of Nabal the Carmelite.

Haifa

Six parasangs from here is Caesarea, the Gath of the Philistines, and here there are about 200 Jews and 200 Cuthim—these are the Jews of Shomron, who are called Samaritans. The city is fair and beautiful, and lies by the sea. It was built by Caesar, and called after him Caesarea. Thence it is half a day's journey to Kako, the Keilah of Scripture. There are no Jews here. Thence it is half a day's journey to St. George, which is Ludd, where there lives one Jew, who is a dyer. Thence it is a day's journey to Sebastiya, which is the city of Shomron (Samaria), and here the ruins of the palace of Ahab, the son of Omri, may be seen. It was formerly a well-fortified city by the mountain-side, with streams of water. It is still a land of brooks, gardens, orchards, vineyards, and olive

Caesarea

Kako

Ludd

Samaria

groves, but no Jews dwell here. Thence it is two parasangs to
Nablus, which is Shechem on Mount Ephraim, where there are
no Jews; the place is situated in the valley between Mount
Gerizim and Mount Ebal, and contains about 1,000 Cuthim, who
observe the written law of Moses alone, and are called Samaritans.
They have priests of the seed (of Aaron), and they call them
Aaronim, who do not intermarry with Cuthim, but wed only
amongst themselves. These priests offer sacrifices, and bring burnt
offerings in their place of assembly on Mount Gerizim, as it is
written in their law—"And thou shalt set the blessing on Mount
Gerizim." They say that this is the proper site of the Temple. On
Passover and the other festivals they offer up burnt offerings on
the altar which they have built on Mount Gerizim, as it is written in their law—"Ye shall set up the stones upon Mount
Gerizim, of the stones which Joshua and the children of Israel set
up at the Jordan." They say that they are descended from the tribe
of Ephraim. And in the midst of them is the grave of Joseph, the
son of Jacob our father, as it is written—"and the bones of Joseph
buried they in Shechem." Their alphabet lacks three letters,
namely ה *He*, ח *Heth*, and ע *Ain*. The letter ה *He* is taken from
Abraham our father, because they have no dignity, the letter ח
Heth from Isaac, because they have no kindliness, and the letter
ע *Ain* from Jacob, because they have no humility. In place of
these letters they make use of the *Aleph*, by which we can tell that
they are not of the seed of Israel, although they know the law of
Moses with the exception of these three letters. They guard
themselves from the defilement of the dead, of the bones of the
slain, and of graves; and they remove the garments which they
have worn before they go to the place of worship, and they bathe
and put on fresh clothes. This is their constant practice. On
Mount Gerizim are fountains and gardens and plantations, but
Mount Ebal is rocky and barren; and between them in the valley
lies the city of Shechem.

It is doubtful whether Benjamin personally visited all the places mentioned in his *Itinerary*. His visit took place not long after the second great Crusade, when Palestine under the kings of Jerusalem was disturbed by internal dissensions and the onslaughts of the Saracens under Nur-ed-din of Damascus, and his generals. Benjamin could at best visit the places of note only when the opportunity offered.

This and most of the other places mentioned by Benjamin are more or less identified in the very important work published by the Palestine Exploration Fund, *The Survey of Western Palestine*. Our author's statements are carefully examined, and Colonel Conder, after expatiating upon the extraordinary mistakes made by writers in the time of the Crusaders, some of whom actually confounded the sea of Galilee with the Mediterranean, says: "The mediaeval Jewish pilgrims appear as a rule to have had a much more accurate knowledge both of the country and of the Bible. Their assertions are borne out by existing remains, and are of the greatest value." [Adler]

From the latter place it is a distance of four parasangs to Mount Gilboa, which the Christians call Mont Gilboa; it lies in a very parched district. And from there it is five parasangs to a village where there are no Jews. Thence it is two parasangs to the valley of Ajalon, which the Christians call Val-de-Luna. At a distance of one parasang is Mahomerie-le-Grand, which is Gibeon the Great; it contains no Jews.

Jerusalem   From there it is three parasangs to Jerusalem, which is a small city, fortified by three walls. It is full of people whom the Mohammedans call Jacobites, Syrians, Greeks, Georgians, and Franks, and of people of all tongues. It contains a dyeing-house, for which the Jews pay a small rent annually to the king, on condition that besides the Jews no other dyers be allowed in Jerusalem. There are about 200 Jews who dwell under the Tower of David in one corner of the city. The lower portion of the wall of the Tower of David, to the extent of about ten cubits, is part of the ancient foundation set up by our ancestors, the remaining portion having been built by the Mohammedans. There is no structure in the whole city stronger than the Tower of David. The city also contains two buildings, from one of which—the hospital—there issue forth four hundred knights [Crusaders]; and therein all the sick who come thither are lodged and cared for in life and in death. The other building is called the Temple of Solomon; it is the palace built by Solomon, the king of Israel. Three hundred knights are quartered there, and issue therefrom every day for military exercise, besides those who come from the land of the Franks and the other parts of Christendom, having taken upon themselves to serve there a year or two until their vow is fulfilled. In Jerusalem is the great church called the Sepulcher, and here is the burial place of Jesus, unto which the Christians make pilgrimages.

Jerusalem has four gates: the Gate of Abraham; the Gate of David; the Gate of Zion; and the Gate of Gushpat, which is the Gate of Jehoshaphat, facing our ancient Temple, now called Templum Domini. Upon the site of the sanctuary Omar ben al Khataab erected an edifice with a very large and magnificent cupola, into which the Gentiles do not bring any image or effigy, but they merely come there to pray. In front of this place is the western wall, which is one of the walls of the Holy of Holies. This is called the Gate of Mercy, and thither come all the Jews to pray before the wall of the court of the Temple. In Jerusalem, attached to the palace which belonged to Solomon, are the stables built by him, forming a very substantial structure, composed of large stones, and the like of it is not to be seen anywhere in the world. There is also visible up to this day the pool used by the priests before offering their sacrifices, and the Jews coming thither write their names upon the wall. The gate of Jehoshaphat leads to the valley of Jehoshaphat, which is the gathering place of nations. Here is the pillar called Absalom's Hand, and the sepulcher of King Uzziah.

In the neighborhood is also a great spring, called the Waters of Siloam, connected with the brook of Kidron. Over the spring is a large structure dating from the time of our ancestors, but little water is found, and the people of Jerusalem for the most part drink the rain water, which they collect in cisterns in their houses. From the valley of Jehoshaphat one ascends the Mount of Olives; it is the valley which separates Jerusalem from the Mount of Olives. From the Mount of Olives one sees the Sea of Sodom [Dead Sea], and at a distance of two parasangs from the Sea of Sodom is the Pillar of Salt into which Lot's wife was turned; the sheep lick it continually, but afterwards it regains its original shape. The whole land of the plain and the valley of Shittim as far as Mount Nebo are visible from here.

In front of Jerusalem is Mount Zion, on which there is no building, except a place of worship belonging to the Christians. Facing Jerusalem for a distance of three miles are the cemeteries belonging to the Israelites, who in the days of old buried their dead in caves, and upon each sepulcher is a dated inscription, but the Christians destroyed the sepulchers, employing the stones thereof in building their houses. These sepulchers reach as far as Zelzah in the territory of Benjamin. Around Jerusalem are high mountains.

On Mount Zion are the sepulchers of the House of David, and the sepulchers of the kings that ruled after him. The exact place cannot be identified, inasmuch as fifteen years ago a wall of the church of Mount Zion fell in. The Patriarch commanded the overseer to take the stones of the old walls and restore therewith the church. He did so, and hired workmen at fixed wages; and there were twenty men who brought the stones from the base of the wall of Zion. Among these men there were two who were sworn friends. On a certain day the one entertained the other; after their meal they returned to their work, when the overseer said to them, "Why have you tarried today?" They answered, "Why need you complain? When our fellow workmen go to their meal we will do our work." When the dinnertime arrived, and the other workmen had gone to their meal, they examined the stones, and raised a certain stone which formed the entrance to a cave. Thereupon one said to the other, "Let us go in and see if any money is to be found there." They entered the cave, and reached a large chamber resting upon pillars of marble overlaid with silver and gold. In front was a table of gold and a scepter and crown. This was the sepulcher of King David. On the left thereof in like fashion was the sepulcher of King Solomon; then followed the sepulcher of all the kings of Judah that were buried there. Closed coffers were also there, the contents of which no man knows. The two men essayed to enter the chamber, when a fierce wind came forth from the entrance of the cave and smote them, and they fell to the ground like dead men, and there they lay until evening. And there came forth a wind like a man's voice, crying out: "Arise and go forth from this place!" So the men rushed forth in terror, and they came unto the Patriarch, and related these things to him. Thereupon the Patriarch sent for Rabbi Abraham el Constantini, the pious recluse, who was one of the mourners of Jerusalem, and to him he related all these things according to the report of the two men who had come forth. Then Rabbi Abraham replied, "These are the sepulchers of the House of David; they belong to the kings of Judah, and on the morrow let us enter, I and you, and these men, and find out what is there." And on the morrow they sent for the two men, and found each of them lying on his bed in terror, and the men said: "We will not enter there, for the Lord doth not desire to show it to any man." Then the Patriarch gave orders that the place should be closed up and hidden from the sight of man unto this day. These things were told me by the said Rabbi Abraham.

Bethlehem   From Jerusalem it is two parasangs to Bethlehem, called by the Christians Beth-Leon, and close thereto, at a distance of about half a mile, at the parting of the way, is the pillar of Rachel's grave, which is made up of eleven stones, corresponding with the number of the sons of Jacob. Upon it is a cupola resting on four columns, and all the Jews that pass by carve their names upon the stones of the pillar. At Bethlehem there are two Jewish dyers. It is a land of brooks of water, and contains wells and fountains.

At a distance of six parasangs is St. Abram de Bron, which is
Hebron   Hebron; the old city stood on the mountain, but is now in ruins; and in the valley by the field of Machpelah lies the present city. Here there is the great church called St. Abram, and this was a Jewish place of worship at the time of the Mohammedan rule, but the Gentiles have erected there six tombs, respectively called those of Abraham and Sarah, Isaac and Rebekah, Jacob and Leah. The custodians tell the pilgrims that these are the tombs of the Patriarchs, for which information the pilgrims give them money. If a Jew comes, however, and gives a special reward, the custodian of the cave opens unto him a gate of iron, which was constructed by our forefathers, and then he is able to descend below by means of steps, holding a lighted candle in his hand. He then reaches a cave, in which nothing is to be found, and a cave beyond, which is likewise empty, but when he reaches the third cave behold there are six sepulchers, those of Abraham, Isaac and Jacob, respectively facing those of Sarah, Rebekah and Leah. And upon the graves are inscriptions cut in stone. Upon the grave of Abraham is engraved "This is the grave of Abraham;" upon that of Isaac, "This is the grave of Isaac, the son of Abraham our

Father;" upon that of Jacob, "This is the grave of Jacob, the son of Isaac, the son of Abraham our Father;" and upon the others, "This is the grave of Sarah," "This is the grave of Rebekah," and "This is the grave of Leah." A lamp burns day and night upon the graves in the cave. One finds there many casks filled with the bones of Israelites, as the members of the house of Israel were wont to bring the bones of their fathers thither and to deposit them there to this day.

Beyond the field of Machpelah is the house of Abraham; there is a well in front of the house, but out of reverence for the Patriarch Abraham no one is allowed to build in the neighborhood.

From Hebron it is five parasangs to Beit Jibrin, which is Mareshah, where there are but three Jews. Three parasangs further one reaches St. Samuel of Shiloh. This is the Shiloh which *Shiloh* is two parasangs from Jerusalem. When the Christians captured Ramlah, the Ramah of old, from the Mohammedans, they found there the grave of Samuel the Ramathite, close to a Jewish synagogue. The Christians took the remains, conveyed them unto Shiloh, and erected over them a large church, and called it St. Samuel of Shiloh unto this day.

> Shiloh, at the time of the Crusaders, was considered to occupy the site of Mizpeh, the highest mountain near Jerusalem, where the national assemblies were held at the time of the Judges. The present mosque is dilapidated, but the substructure, which dates from the Frank period, is beautifully jointed. The apse is raised. The reputed tomb of Samuel is on the western side of the church. It is still called Nebi Samwil, venerated alike by Jew and Moslem. [Adler]

From there it is three parasangs to Mahomerie-le-petit, which is Gibeah of Saul, where there are no Jews, and this is Gibeah of Benjamin. Thence three parasangs to Beit Nuba, which is Nob, the city of priests. In the middle of the way are the two crags of

Jonathan, the name of the one being Bozez, and the name of the other Seneh. Two Jewish dyers dwell there.

> Beit-Nuba near Ramleh has been identified without proof with Nob. Richard Coeur-de-Lion encamped here some twenty-five years after Benjamin's visit. He, with the army of the Crusaders, passed through Ibelin on his way to Askelon. [Adler]

Ramleh   Thence it is three parasangs to Rams, or Ramleh, where there are remains of the walls from the days of our ancestors, for thus it was found written upon the stones. About 300 Jews dwell there. It was formerly a very great city; at a distance of two miles there is a large Jewish cemetery.

> Ramleh did not exist in Bible times—it was founded in 716. It prospered to such an extent that it became as large as Jerusalem. It was a good deal damaged by an earthquake in 1033. Ramleh had a large Moslem population, and the Jews there remained comparatively unmolested by the Crusaders. This latter fact accounts for the somewhat large number of Jews residing there. [Adler]

Jaffa   Thence it is five parasangs to Yāfa or Jaffa, which is on the seaboard, and one Jewish dyer lives here. From here it is five parasangs to Ibelin or Jabneh, the seat of the Academy, but there are no Jews there at this day. Thus far extends the territory of Ephraim.

Ashdod   From there it is five parasangs to Palmid, which is Ashdod of the Philistines, now in ruins; no Jews dwell there. Thence it is

Askelon   two parasangs to Ashkelonah or New Askelon, which Ezra the priest built by the sea. It was originally called Bene Berak. The place is four parasangs distant from the ancient ruined city of Askelon. New Askelon is a large and fair place, and merchants come thither from all quarters, for it is situated on the frontier of Egypt. About 200 Rabbanite Jews dwell here, at their head being R. Zemach, R. Aaron, and R. Solomon; also about forty Karaïtes, and about 300 Cuthim. In the midst of the city there is a well, which they call Bir Abraham; this the Patriarch dug in the days of the Philistines.

From there it is a journey of a day to St. George of Ludd— thence it is a day and a half to Zerin or Jezreel, where there is a large spring. One Jewish dyer lives here. Three parasangs further is Saffuriya or Sepphoris. Here are the graves of Rabbenu Hakkadosh (R. Judah the Prince), of Rabban Gamaliel, and of R. Chiya, who came up from Babylon, also of Jonah the son of Amittai; they are all buried in the mountain. Many other Jewish graves are here. *Jezreel*

Sepphoris

Thence it is five parasangs to Tiberias, which is situated upon the Jordan, which is here called the Sea of Chinnereth. The Jordan at this place flows through a valley between two mountains, and fills the lake, which is called the Lake of Chinnereth; this is a large and broad piece of water, like the sea. The Jordan flows between two mountains, and over the plain which is the place that is called Ashdoth Hapisgah, and thence continues its course till it falls into the Sea of Sodom, which is the Salt Sea. In Tiberias there are about fifty Jews, at their head being R. Abraham the astronomer, R. Muchtar, and R. Isaac. There are hot waters here, which bubble up from the ground, and are called the Hot Waters of Tiberias. Nearby is the Synagogue of Caleb ben Jephunneh, and Jewish sepulchers. R. Johanan ben Zakkai and R. Jehudah Halevi are buried here. All these places are situated in Lower Galilee. *Tiberius/ Sea of Kinnereth*

From here it is two days to Tymin or Timnathah, where Simon the Just and many Israelites are buried, and thence three parasangs to Medon or Meron. In the neighborhood there is a cave in which are the sepulchers of Hillel and Shammai. Here also are twenty sepulchers of disciples, including the sepulchers of R. Benjamin ben Japheth, and of R. Jehudah ben Bethera. From Meron it is *Tymin*

Meron

Almah   two parasangs to Almah, where there are about fifty Jews. There is a large Jewish cemetery here, with the sepulchers of R. Eleazar ben Arak, of R. Eleazar ben Azariah, of Chuni Hamaagal, of Raban Simeon ben Gamaliel, and of R. Jose Hagelili.

Kades   From here it is half a day's journey to Kades, or Kedesh Naphtali, upon the Jordan. Here is the sepulcher of Barak, the son of Abinoam. No Jews dwell here.

Banias   Thence it is a day's journey to Banias, which is Dan, where there is a cavern, from which the Jordan issues and flows for a distance of three miles, when the Arnon, which comes from the borders of Moab, joins it. In front of the cavern may be discerned the site of the altar associated with the graven image of Micah, which the children of Dan worshipped in ancient days. This is also the site of the altar of Jeroboam, where the golden calf was set up. Thus far reaches the boundary of the land of Israel towards the uttermost sea.

Damascus   Two days' journey brings one to Damascus, the great city, which is the commencement of the empire of Nur-ed-din, the king of the Togarmim, called Turks. It is a fair city of large extent, surrounded by walls, with many gardens and plantations, extending over fifteen miles on each side, and no district richer in fruit can be seen in all the world. From Mount Hermon descend the rivers Amana and Pharpar; for the city is situated at the foot of Mount Hermon. The Amana flows through the city, and by means of aqueducts the water is conveyed to the houses of the great people, and into the streets and market places. The Pharpar flows through their gardens and plantations. It is a place carrying on trade with all countries. Here is a mosque of the Arabs called the Gami of Damascus; there is no building like it in the whole world, and they say that it was a palace of Ben Hadad. Here is a wall of crystal glass of magic workmanship, with apertures according to the days of the year, and as the sun's rays enter each

« 90 »

of them in daily succession the hours of the day can be told by a graduated dial. In the palace are chambers built of gold and glass, and if people walk round the wall they are able to see one another, although the wall is between them. And there are columns overlaid with gold and silver, and columns of marble of all colours. And in the court there is a gigantic head overlaid with gold and silver, and fashioned like a bowl with rims of gold and silver. It is as big as a cask, and three men can enter therein at the same time to bathe. In the palace is suspended the rib of one of the giants, the length being nine cubits, and the width two cubits; and they say it belonged to the King Anak of the giants of old, whose name was Abramaz. For so it was found inscribed on his grave, where it was also written that he ruled over the whole world. Three thousand Jews abide in this city, and amongst them are learned and rich men. The head of the Academy of the land of Israel resides here. His name is R. Azariah, and with him are his brother, Sar Shalom, the head of the Beth Din; R. Joseph, the fifth of the Academy; R. Mazliach, the lecturer, the head of the order; R. Meir, the crown of the scholars; R. Joseph ben Al Pilath, the pillar of the Academy; R. Heman, the warden; and R. Zedekiah, the physician. One hundred Karaïtes dwell here, also 400 Cuthim, and there is peace between them, but they do not intermarry.

It is a day's journey to Galid, which is Gilead, and sixty *Gilead* Israelites are there, at their head being R. Zadok, R. Isaac, and R. Solomon. It is a place of wide extent, with brooks of water, gardens, and plantations. Thence it is half a day to Salkat, which is Salchah of old.

Thence it is half a day's journey to Baalbec, which is Baalath *Baalbec* in the plains of Lebanon, and which Solomon built for the daughter of Pharaoh. The palace is built of large stones, each stone having a length of twenty cubits and a width of twelve cubits, and there are no spaces between the stones. It is said that Ashmedai alone could have put up this building. From the upper part of the city a great spring wells forth and flows into the middle of the city as a wide stream, and alongside thereof are mills and gardens and plantations in the midst of the city. At Tarmod

Tadmor (Tadmor) in the wilderness, which Solomon built, there are similar structures of huge stones. The city of Tarmod is surrounded by walls; it is in the desert far away from inhabited places, and is four days' journey from Baalath, just mentioned. And in Tarmod there are about 2,000 Jews. They are valiant in war and fight with the Christians and with the Arabs, which latter are under the dominion of Nur-ed-din the king, and they help their neighbors, the Ishmaelites. At their head are R. Isaac Hajvani, R. Nathan, and R. Uziel.

From Baalbec to Karjatēn, which is Kirjathim, is a distance of half a day; no Jews live there except one dyer. Thence it is a day's

Emesa journey to Emesa, which is a city of the Zemarites, where about twenty Jews dwell. Thence it is a day's journey to Hamah, which is Hamath. It lies on the river Jabbok, at the foot of Mount Lebanon.

The important city Emesa, now called Homs, is here probably indicated. In Scripture, Gen. x. 18, the Zemarite and the Hamathite are grouped together among the Canaanite families. In this district is the intermittent spring of Fuwâr ed-Der, the Sabbatio River of antiquity, which Titus visited after the destruction of Jerusalem. Josephus describes it as follows: "Its current is strong and has plenty of water; after which its springs fail for six days together and leave its channels dry, as any one may see; after which days it runs on the seventh day as it did before, and as though it had undergone no change at all. It has also been observed to keep this order perpetually and exactly." The intermittent action is readily accounted for by the stream having hollowed out an underground duct, which acts as a siphon.

Hamath is often mentioned in Scripture, situated at no great distance from the Orontes. In the troublous time after the first crusade it was taken by the Ismailians or Assassins. The earthquake of 1157 caused great damage. Twenty years later the place was captured by Saladin. [Adler]

Some time ago there was a great earthquake in the city, and 25,000 souls perished in one day, and of about 200 Jews but seventy escaped. At their head are R. Eli Hacohen, and the Sheik Abu Galib and Mukhtar. Thence it is half a day to Sheizar, which is Hazor, and from there it is three parasangs to Dimin (Latmin).

Thence it is two days to Haleb (Aleppo) or Aram Zoba, which *Aleppo* is the royal city of Nur-ed-din. In the midst of the city is his palace surrounded by a very high wall. This is a very large place. There is no well there nor any stream, but the inhabitants drink rain water, each one possessing a cistern in his house. The city has 5,000 Jewish inhabitants, at their head being R. Moses el Constantini and R. Seth. Thence it is two days to Balis, which is *Balis* Pethor on the river Euphrates, and unto this day there stands the turret of Balaam, which he built to tell the hours of the day. About ten Jews live here. Thence it is half a day to Kalat Jabar, *Kalat Jabar* which is Selah of the wilderness, that was left unto the Arabs at the time the Togarmim took their land and caused them to fly into the wilderness. About 2,000 Jews dwell there, at their head being R. Zedekiah, R. Chiya, and R. Solomon.

Thence it is one day's journey to Rakka, or Salchah, which is *Rakka* on the confines of the land of Shinar, and which divides the land of the Togarmim from that kingdom. In it there are 700 Jews, at their head being R. Zakkai and R. Nedib, who is blind, and R. Joseph. There is a synagogue here, erected by Ezra when he went forth from Babylon to Jerusalem. At two days' distance lies ancient Harrān, where twenty Jews live. Here is another syna- *Harrān* gogue erected by Ezra, and in this place stood the house of Terah and Abraham, his son. The ground is not covered by any building, and the Mohammedans honour the site and come thither to pray.

Ras-el-Ain Thence it is a journey of two days to Ras-el-Ain, whence proceeds the river El Khabur—the Habor of old—which flows through the land of Media, and falls into the river Gozan. Here

Geziret Omar there are 200 Jews. Thence it is two days to Geziret Ibn Omar, which is surrounded by the river Hiddekel (Tigris), at the foot of the mountains of Ararat.

It is a distance of four miles to the place where Noah's Ark rested, but Omar ben al Khataab took the ark from the two mountains and made it into a mosque for the Mohammedans.

Josephus mentions that Noah's Ark still existed in his day. Rabbi Pethachia, who travelled through Armenia within twenty years after Benjamin, speaks of four mountain peaks, between which the Ark became fixed and from which it could not get free. [Adler]

Near the ark is the Synagogue of Ezra to this day, and on the ninth of Ab the Jews come thither from the city to pray. In the city of Geziret Omar are 4,000 Jews, at their head being R. Mubchar, R. Joseph and R. Chiya.

Mosul Thence it is two days to Mosul, which is Assur the Great, and here dwell about 7,000 Jews, at their head being R. Zakkai the Nasi, of the seed of David, and R. Joseph, surnamed Burhan-al-mulk, the astronomer to the King Sin-ed-din, the brother of Nur-ed-din, King of Damascus. Mosul is the frontier town of the land of Persia. It is a very large and ancient city, situated on the river Hiddekel (Tigris), and is connected with Nineveh by means of a bridge. Nineveh is in ruins, but amid the ruins there are villages and hamlets, and the extent of the city may be determined by the walls, which extend forty parasangs to the city of Irbil. The city of Nineveh is on the river Hiddekel. In the city of Assur (Mosul)

is the Synagogue of Obadiah, built by Jonah; also the Synagogue
of Nahum the Elkoshite.

Thence it is a distance of three days to Rahbah, which is on the *Rahbah*
river Euphrates. Here there are about 2,000 Jews, at their head
being R. Hezekiah, R. Tahor and R. Isaac. It is a very fine city,
large and fortified, and surrounded by gardens and plantations.

Thence it is a day's journey to Karkisiya which is Carchemish, *Karkisiya*
on the river Euphrates. Here there are about 500 Jews, at their
head being R. Isaac and R. Elhanan. Thence it is two days to El-
Anbar which is Pumbedita in Nehardea. Here reside 3,000 Jews, *El-Anbar*
and amongst them are learned men, at their head being the chief
rabbi R. Chen, R. Moses, and R. Jehoiakim. Here are the graves
of Rab Jehuda and Samuel, and in front of the graves of each of
them are the synagogues which they built in their lifetime. Here
is also the grave of Bostanai the Nasi, the head of the Captivity,
and of R. Nathan and Rab Nachman, the son of Papa.

Thence it takes five days to Hadara, where about 15,000 Jews *Hadara*
dwell, at their head being R. Zaken, R. Jehosef, and R. Nethanel.

Thence it takes two days to Okbara, the city which Jeconiah *Okbara*
the King built, where there are about 10,000 Jews, and at their
head are R. Chanan, R. Jabin, and R. Ishmael.

Thence it is two days to Baghdad, the great city and the royal *Baghdad*
residence of the Caliph Emir al Muminin al Abbasi of the family
of Mohammed. He is at the head of the Mohammedan religion,
and all the kings of Islam obey him; he occupies a similar position to that held by the Pope over the Christians.

The Caliphs of the Abbaside Dynasty traced their descent from
Mohammed. Benjamin here refers to the Caliph El Mostanshed. The
Caliph is aptly compared to the Pope. In addition to his temporal authority
at Baghdad, he exercised as Leader of the Faithful—Emir al-Muminin—
religious authority over all Mohammedans from Spain to India. At a later
time the vizier arrogated all authority to himself, and the Caliph spent his
time either in the mosque or in the seraglio. [Adler]

He has a palace in Baghdad three miles in extent, wherein is a great park with all varieties of trees, fruit bearing and otherwise, and all manner of animals. The whole is surrounded by a wall, and in the park there is a lake whose waters are fed by the river Hiddekel. Whenever the king desires to indulge in recreation and to rejoice and feast, his servants catch all manner of birds, game and fish, and he goes to his palace with his counsellors and princes. There the great king, Al Abbasi the Caliph (Hafiz) holds his court, and he is kind unto Israel, and many belonging to the people of Israel are his attendants; he knows all languages, and is well versed in the law of Israel. He reads and writes the holy language (Hebrew). He will not partake of anything unless he has earned it by the work of his own hands. He makes coverlets to which he attaches his seal; his courtiers sell them in the market, and the great ones of the land purchase them, and the proceeds thereof provide his sustenance. He is truthful and trusty, speaking peace to all men. The men of Islam see him but once in the year. The pilgrims that come from distant lands to go unto Mecca, which is in the land El-Yemen, are anxious to see his face, and they assemble before the palace exclaiming, "Our Lord, light of Islam and glory of our Law, show us the effulgence of thy countenance"—but he pays no regard to their words. Then the princes who minister unto him say to him, "Our Lord, spread forth thy peace unto the men that have come from distant lands, who crave to abide under the shadow of thy graciousness." Thereupon he arises and lets down the hem of his robe from the window, and the pilgrims come and kiss it, and a prince says unto them, "Go forth in peace, for our Master, the Lord of Islam, granteth peace to you." He is regarded by them as Mohammed, and they go to their houses rejoicing at the salutation which the prince has vouchsafed unto them, and glad at heart that they have kissed his robe.

Each of his brothers and the members of his family has an abode in his palace, but they are all fettered in chains of iron, and guards are placed over each of their houses so that they may not rise against the great Caliph. For once it happened to a predecessor that his brothers rose up against him and proclaimed one of themselves as Caliph; then it was decreed that all the members of his family should be bound, that they might not rise up against the ruling Caliph. Each one of them resides in his palace in great splendour, and they own villages and towns, and their stewards bring them the tribute thereof, and they eat and drink and rejoice all the days of their life.

Within the domains of the palace of the Caliph there are great buildings of marble and columns of silver and gold, and carvings upon rare stones are fixed in the walls. In the Caliph's palace are great riches, and towers filled with gold, silken garments, and all precious stones. He does not issue forth from his palace save once in the year, at the feast which the Mohammedans call El-id-bed Ramazan, and they come from distant lands that day to see him. He rides on a mule and is attired in the royal robes of gold and silver and fine linen; on his head is a turban adorned with precious stones of priceless value, and over the turban is a black shawl as a sign of his modesty, implying that all this glory will be covered by darkness on the day of death. He is accompanied by all the nobles of Islam dressed in fine garments and riding on horses, the princes of Arabia, the princes of Togarma and Daylam (Gilan), and the princes of Persia, Media and Ghuzz, and the princes of the land of Tibet, which is three months' journey distant, and westward of which lies the land of Samarkand. He proceeds from his palace to the great mosque of Islam, which is by the Basrah Gate. Along the road the walls are adorned with silk and purple, and the inhabitants receive him with all kinds of song and exultation, and they dance before the great king who is styled the Caliph. They salute him with a loud voice and say: "Peace unto thee, our Lord, the King and Light of Islam!" He kisses his robe, and stretching forth the hem thereof he salutes them. Then he proceeds to the court of the mosque, mounts a wooden pulpit and expounds to them their Law. Then the learned ones of Islam arise and pray for him and extol his greatness and his graciousness, to which they all respond. Afterwards he gives them his blessing, and they bring before him a camel which he slays, and this is their passover-sacrifice. He gives thereof unto the princes and they distribute it to all, so that they may taste of the sacrifice brought by their sacred king; and they all rejoice. Afterwards he leaves the mosque and returns alone to his palace by way of the river Hiddekel, and the grandees of Islam accompany him in ships on the river until he enters his palace. He does not return the way he came; and the road which he takes along the riverside is watched all the year through, so that no man shall tread in his footsteps. He does not leave the palace again for a whole year. He is a benevolent man.

He built, on the other side of the river, on the banks of an arm of the Euphrates which there borders the city, a hospital consisting of blocks of houses and hospices for the sick poor who come to be healed. Here there are about sixty physicians' stores which are provided from the Caliph's house with drugs and whatever else may be required. Every sick man who comes is maintained at the Caliph's expense and is medically treated. Here is a building which is called Dar-al-Maristan, where they keep charge of the demented people who have become insane in the towns through the great heat in the summer, and they chain each of them in iron chains until their reason becomes restored to them in the winter-time. Whilst they abide there, they are provided with food from the house of the Caliph, and when their reason is restored they are dismissed and each one of them goes to his house and his home. Money is given to those that have stayed in the hospices on their return to their homes. Every month the officers of the Caliph inquire and investigate whether they have regained their reason, in which case they are discharged. All this the Caliph does out of charity to those that come to the city of Baghdad, whether they be sick or insane. The Caliph is a righteous man, and all his actions are for good.

In Baghdad there are about 40,000 Jews, and they dwell in security, prosperity and honour under the great Caliph; and amongst them are great sages, the heads of Academies engaged in the study of the law. In this city there are ten Academies. At the head of the Great Academy is the chief rabbi R. Samuel, the son of Eli. He is the Head of the Academy, Gaon Jacob. He is a Levite, and traces his pedigree back to Moses, our teacher. The head of the second Academy is R. Hanania, his brother, warden of the Levites. R. Daniel is the head of the third Academy. R. Elazar, the scholar, is the head of the fourth Academy; and R. Elazar, the son of Zemach, is the head of the order, and his pedigree reaches to Samuel the prophet, the Korahite. He and his brethren know how to chant the melodies as did the singers at the time when the Temple was standing. He is head of the sixth Academy. R. Haggai is head of the seventh Academy. R. Ezra is the head of the eighth Academy. R. Abraham, who is called Abu Tahir, is the head of the ninth Academy. R. Zakkai, the son of Bostanai the Nasi, is the head of the Sium [tenth]. These are the ten Batlanim, and they do not engage in any other work than communal administration; and all the days of the week they judge the Jews, their countrymen, except on the second day of the week, when they all appear before the chief rabbi, Samuel, the Head of the Yeshiba Gaon Jacob, who in conjunction with the other Batlanim judges all those that appear before him. And at the head of them all is Daniel, the son of Hisdai, who is styled, "Our Lord, the Head of the Captivity of all Israel." He possesses a book of pedigrees going back as far as David, King of Israel. The Jews call him, "Our Lord, Head of the Captivity," and the Mohammedans call him, "Saidna ben Daoud," and he has been invested with authority over all the congregations of Israel at the hands of the Emir al Muminin, the Lord of Islam. For thus Mohammed commanded concerning him and his descendants; and he granted him a seal of office over all the congregations that dwell under his rule, and ordered that every one, whether Mohammedan or Jew, or belonging to any other nation in his dominion, should rise up before him (the Exilarch) and salute him, and that any one who should refuse to rise up should receive one hundred stripes.

The office of Exilarch had but recently been revived, and the Mohammed here referred to may have been Mohammed El Moktafi, the Caliph Mostanshed's predecessor. [Adler]

And every fifth day when he goes to pay a visit to the great Caliph, horsemen, Gentiles as well as Jews, escort him, and heralds proclaim in advance, "Make way before our Lord, the son of David, as is due unto him," the Arabic words being "Amilu tarik la Saidna ben Daud." He is mounted on a horse, and is attired in robes of silk and embroidery, with a large turban on his head, and from the turban is suspended a long white cloth adorned with a chain upon which the cipher of Mohammed is engraved. Then he appears before the Caliph and kisses his hand, and the Caliph rises and places him on a throne which Mohammed had ordered to be made for him, and all the Mohammedan princes who attend the court of the Caliph rise up before him. And the Head of the Captivity is seated on his throne opposite to the Caliph, in compliance with the command of Mohammed, to give effect to what is written in the law—"The scepter shall not depart from Judah nor a law-giver from between his feet, until he come to Shiloh: and to him shall the gathering of the people be." The authority of the Head of the Captivity extends over all the communities of Shinar, Persia, Khurasan, and Sheba which is El-Yemen [Arabia], and Diyar Kalach (Bekr) and the land of Aram

Naharaim (Mesopotamia), and over the dwellers in the mountains of Ararat and the land of the Alans [Caucasus], which is a land surrounded by mountains and has no outlet except by the iron gates which Alexander made, but which were afterwards broken. Here are the people called Alani. His authority extends also over the land of Siberia, and the communities in the land of the Togarmim unto the mountains of Asveh and the land of Gurgan, the inhabitants of which are called Gurganim who dwell by the river Gihon [Oxus], and these are the Girgashites who follow the [Nestorian] Christian religion. Further it extends to the gates of Samarkand, the land of Tibet, and the land of India. In respect of all these countries the Head of the Captivity gives the communities power to appoint Rabbis and Ministers who come unto him to be consecrated and to receive his authority. They bring him offerings and gifts from the ends of the earth. He owns hospices, gardens and plantations in Babylon, and much land inherited from this fathers, and no one can take his possessions from him by force. He has a fixed weekly revenue arising from the hospices of the Jews, the markets and the merchants, apart from that which is brought to him from far off lands. The man is very rich and wise in the Scriptures as well as in the Talmud, and many Israelites dine at his table every day.

At his installation, the Head of the Captivity gives much money to the Caliph, to the Princes and the Ministers. On the day that the Caliph performs the ceremony of investing him with authority, he rides in the second of the royal equipages, and is escorted from the palace of the Caliph to his own house with timbrels and fifes. The Exilarch appoints the Chiefs of the Academies by placing his hand upon their heads, thus installing them in their office. The Jews of the city are learned men, and very rich.

In Baghdad there are twenty-eight Jewish synagogues, situated either in the city itself or in Al-Karkh on the other side of the Tigris; for the river divides the metropolis into two parts. The great synagogue of the Head of the Captivity has columns of marble of various colours overlaid with silver and gold, and on these columns are sentences of the Psalms in golden letters. And in front of the ark are about ten steps of marble; on the topmost step are the seats of the Head of the Captivity and of the Princes of the House of David. The city of Baghdad is twenty miles in circumference, situated in a land of palms, gardens, and plantations, the like of which is not to be found in the whole land of Shinar. People come thither with merchandise from all lands. Wise men live there, philosophers who know all manner of wisdom, and magicians expert in all manner of witchcraft.

Resen   Thence it is two days to Gazigan, which is called Resen. It is a large city containing about 5,000 Jews. In the midst of it is the Synagogue of Rabbah—a large one. He is buried close to the synagogue, and beneath his sepulcher is a cave where twelve of his pupils are buried.

Babylon   Thence it is a day's journey to Babylon, which is the Babel of old. The ruins thereof are thirty miles in extent. The ruins of the palace of Nebuchadnezzar are still to be seen there, but people are afraid to enter them on account of the serpents and scorpions. Near at hand, within a distance of a mile, there dwell 3,000 Israelites who pray in the Synagogue of the Pavilion of Daniel, which is ancient, and was erected by Daniel. It is built of hewn stones and bricks. Between the synagogue and the Palace of Nebuchadnezzar is the furnace into which were thrown Hananiah, Mishael, and Azariah, and the site of it lies in a valley known unto all.

The Babel of Bible times was captured by Sennacherib; after stopping up a dam of the Euphrates, the country was placed under water and the city destroyed. Nebuchadnezzar restored the city; he also erected a magnificent palace for himself—the Kasr—also the Temple of Bel. Herodotus fully describes these edifices, and dwells upon the huge extent of the metropolis, which was estimated to have a circuit of fifty miles. Xerxes destroyed the city. Alexander the Great contemplated the restoration of Bel's Temple, but as it would have taken two months for 10,000 men merely to remove the rubbish, he abandoned the attempt. The ruins have been recently explored by Germans. The embankments which regulated the flow of the Euphrates and Tigris have given way, and at the present time the whole region around Babylon is marshy and malarious. In the words of Jeremiah, li. 43, "Her cities are a desolation, a sterile land, and a wilderness, a place wherein no man dwelleth." [Adler]

Thence it is five parasangs to Hillah, where there are 10,000 *Hillah* Israelites, and four synagogues: that of R. Meir, who lies buried before it; the Synagogue of Mar Keshisha, who is buried in front of it; also the Synagogue of Rab Zeiri, the son of Chama; and the Synagogue of R. Mari—the Jews pray there every day.

Thence it is four miles to the Tower of Babel, which the generation whose language was confounded, built of the bricks called Agur. The length of its foundation is about two miles, the breadth of the tower is about forty cubits, and the length thereof two hundred cubits. At every ten cubits' distance there are slopes which go round the tower by which one can ascend to the top. One can see from there a view twenty miles in extent, as the land is level. There fell fire from heaven into the midst of the tower which split it to its very depths.

Thence it is half a day to Kaphri, where there are about 200 *Kaphri* Jews. Here is the Synagogue of R. Isaac Napcha, who is buried in front of it. Thence it is three parasangs to the Synagogue of Ezekiel, the prophet of blessed memory, which is by the river Euphrates. It is fronted by sixty turrets, and between each turret there is a minor synagogue, and in the court of the synagogue is the ark, and at the back of the synagogue is the sepulcher of Ezekiel. It is surmounted by a large cupola, and it is a very handsome structure. It was built of old by King Jeconiah, king of

Judah, and the 35,000 Jews who came with him, when Evil-merodach brought him forth out of prison. This place is by the river Chebar on the one side and by the river Euphrates on the other, and the names of Jeconiah and those that accompanied him are engraved on the wall: Jeconiah at the top, and Ezekiel at the bottom. This place is held sacred by Israel as a lesser sanctuary unto this day, and people come from a distance to pray there from the time of the New Year until the Day of Atonement. The Israelites have great rejoicings on these occasions. Thither also come the Head of the Captivity, and the Heads of the Academies from Baghdad. Their camp occupies a space of about two miles, and Arab merchants come there as well. A great gathering like a fair takes place, which is called Fera, and they bring forth a scroll of the Law written on parchment by Ezekiel the Prophet, and read from it on the Day of Atonement. A lamp burns day and night over the sepulcher of Ezekiel; the light thereof has been kept burning from the day that he lighted it himself, and they continually renew the wick thereof, and replenish the oil unto the present day. A large house belonging to the sanctuary is filled with books, some of them from the time of the first temple, and some from the time of the second temple, and he who has no sons consecrates his books to its use. The Jews that come thither to pray from the lands of Persia and Media bring the money which their countrymen have offered to the Synagogue of Ezekiel the Prophet. The synagogue owns property, lands, and villages, which belonged to King Jeconiah, and when Mohammed came he confirmed all these rights to the Synagogue of Ezekiel. Distinguished Mohammedans also come hither to pray, so great is their love for Ezekiel the Prophet; and they call it Bar (Dar) Melicha (the Dwelling of Beauty). All the Arabs come there to pray.

At a distance of about half a mile from the synagogue are the sepulchers of Hananiah, Mishael, and Azariah, and upon their sepulchers are large cupolas; and even at times of disturbance no man would dare touch the Mohammedan or Jewish servants who attend at the sepulcher of Ezekiel.

Thence it is three miles to the city of Kotsonath, where there are 300 Jews. Here are the sepulchers of Rab Papa, Rab Huna, Joseph Sinai, and Rab Joseph ben Hama; and before each of them is a synagogue where the Israelites pray every day. Thence it is three parasangs to Ain Sipha, where there is the sepulcher of the prophet Nahum the Elkoshite. Thence it is a day's journey to Kefar Al-Keram, where are the sepulchers of Rab Chisdai, R. Azariah, R. Akiba, and R. Dosa. Thence it is a half-day's journey to a village in the desert, where there are buried R. David and R. Jehuda and Abaji, R. Kurdiah, Rab Sechora, and Rab Ada. Thence it is a day's journey to the river Raga, where there is the sepulcher of King Zedekiah. Upon it is a large cupola. Thence it is a day's journey to the city of Kufa, where there is the sepulcher of King Jeconiah. Over it is a big structure, and in front thereof is a synagogue. There are about 7,000 Jews here. At this place is the large mosque of the Mohammedans, for here is buried Ali ben Abu Talib, the son-in-law of Mohammed, and the Mohammedans come hither.

Thence it is a day and a half to Sura, which is Mata Mehasya, where the Heads of the Captivity and the Heads of the Academies dwelt at first. Here is the sepulcher of R. Sherira, and of R. Hai, his son of blessed memory. Also of R. Saadiah Al-Fayummi, and of Rab Samuel, the son of Hofni HaCohen, and of Zephaniah, the son of Cushi, the son of Gedaliah the prophet, and of the Princes of the House of David, and of the Heads of the Academies who lived there before the destruction of the town.

Thence it is two days to Shafjathib. Here is a synagogue which the Israelites built from the earth of Jerusalem and its stones, and they called it Shafjathib, which is by Nehardea.

Thence it is a day and a half's journey to El-Anbar, which was

Kotsonath

Kufa

Sura

El-Anbar

« 105 »

Pumbedita in Nehardea. About 3,000 Jews dwell there. The city lies on the river Euphrates. Here is the Synagogue of Rab and Samuel, and their house of study, and in front of it are their graves.

Thence it is five days to Hillah. From this place it is a journey of twenty-one days by way of the deserts to the land of Saba, *Yemen/* which is called the land El-Yemen, lying at the side of the land *Arabia* of Shinar which is towards the North.

Teima Here dwell the Jews called Kheibar, the men of Teima. And Teima is their seat of government where R. Hanan the Nasi rules over them. It is a great city, and the extent of their land is sixteen days' journey. It is surrounded by mountains—the mountains of the north. The Jews own many large fortified cities. The yoke of the Gentiles is not upon them. They go forth to pillage and to capture booty from distant lands in conjunction with the Arabs, their neighbors and allies. These Arabs dwell in tents, and they make the desert their home. They own no houses, and they go forth to pillage and to capture booty in the land of Shinar and El-Yemen. All the neighbors of these Jews go in fear of them. Among them are husbandmen and owners of cattle; their land is extensive, and they have in their midst learned and wise men. They give the tithe of all they possess unto the scholars who sit in the house of learning, also to poor Israelites and to the recluses, who are the Mourners of Zion and Jerusalem, and who do not eat meat nor taste wine, and sit clad in garments of black. They dwell in caves or underground houses, and fast each day, with the exception of the Sabbaths and Festivals, and implore mercy of the Holy One, blessed be He, on account of the exile of Israel, praying that He may take pity upon them, and upon all the Jews, the men of Teima, for the sake of His great Name; also upon *Tilmas* Tilmas, the great city, in which there are about 100,000 Jews. At this place lives Salmon the Nasi, the brother of Hanan the Nasi;

and the land belongs to the two brothers, who are of the seed of David, for they have their pedigree in writing. They address many questions unto the Head of the Captivity—their kinsman in Baghdad—and they fast forty days in the year for the Jews that dwell in exile.

There are here about forty large towns and 200 hamlets and villages. The principle city is Tanai, and in all the districts together *Tanai* there are about 300,000 Jews. The city of Tanai is well fortified, and in the midst thereof the people sow and reap. It is fifteen miles in extent. Here is the palace of the Nasi called Salmon. And in Teima dwells Hanan the Nasi, his brother. It is a beautiful city, and contains gardens and plantations. And Tilmas is likewise a great city; it contains about 100,000 Jews. It is well fortified, and is situated between two high mountains. There are wise, discreet, and rich men amongst the inhabitants. From Tilmas to Kheibar it is three days' journey. People say that the men of Kheibar belong to the tribes of Reuben, Gad, and Manasseh, whom Shalmaneser, king of Assyria, led hither into captivity. They have built strongly-fortified cities, and make war upon all other kingdoms. No man can readily reach their territory, because it is a march of eighteen days' journey through the desert, which is altogether uninhabited, so that no one can enter the land.

Kheibar is a very large city, with 50,000 Jews. In it are learned *Kheibar* men, and great warriors, who wage war with the men of Shinar and of the land of the north, as well as with the bordering tribes of the land of El-Yemen near them, which latter country is on the confines of India. Returning from their land, it is a journey of twenty-five days to the river Virae, which is in the land of El-Yemen, where about 3,000 Jews dwell, and amongst them are many a Rabbi and Dayan.

It will be seen further on that Benjamin speaks of Aden as being in India, "which is on the mainland." It is well known that Abyssinia and Arabia were in the Middle Ages spoken of as "Middle India." It has been ascertained that in ancient times the Arabs extensively colonized the western seacoast of the East Indies. [Adler]

Basra Thence it takes five days to Basra (Bassorah) which lies on the river Tigris. Here there are 10,000 Jews, and among them are scholars and many rich men. Thence it is two days to the river *Persia* Samara, which is the commencement of the land of Persia. Fifteen hundred Jews live near the sepulcher of Ezra, the priest, who went forth from Jerusalem to King Artaxerxes, and died there. In front of his sepulcher is a large synagogue. And at the side thereof the Mohammedans erected a house of prayer out of their great love and veneration for him, and they like the Jews on that account. And the Mohammedans come hither to pray.

Khuzistan Thence it is four days to Khuzistan, which is Elam. This province is not inhabited in its entirety, for part of it lies waste. In the *Susa* midst of its ruins is Shushan (Susa), the capital, the site of the palace of King Ahasuerus. Here are the remains of a large structure of great antiquity. The city contains about 7,000 Jews and fourteen synagogues.

In front of one of the synagogues is the sepulcher of Daniel, of blessed memory. The river Tigris divides the city, and the bridge connects the two parts. On the one side where the Jews dwell is the sepulcher of Daniel. Here the market-places used to be, containing great stores of merchandise, by which the Jews became enriched. On the other side of the bridge they were poor, because they had no market-places nor merchants there, only gardens and plantations. And they became jealous, and said, "All this prosperity enjoyed by those on the other side is due to the merits of Daniel the prophet who lies buried there." Then the poor people asked those who dwelt on the other side to place the sepulcher of Daniel in their midst, but the others would not comply. So war prevailed between them for many days, and no one went forth or came in on account of the great strife between them. At length both parties growing tired of this state of things took a wise view of the matter, and made a compact, namely, that the coffin of Daniel should be taken for one year to the one side and for another year to the other side. This they did, and both sides became rich. In the course of time Sinjar Shah-ben-Shah, who ruled over the kingdom of Persia and had forty-five kings subject to his authority, came to this place.

He is called Sultan-al-Fars-al-Khabir in Arabic (the mighty Sovereign of Persia), and it is he who ruled from the river Samara unto the city of Samarkand, and unto the river Gozan, and the cities of Media, and the mountains of Chafton. He ruled also over Tibet, in the forests whereof one finds the animals from which the musk is obtained. The extent of his Empire is a journey of four months. When this great Emperor Sinjar, king of Persia, saw that they took the coffin of Daniel from one side of the river to the other, and that a great multitude of Jews, Mohammedans, and Gentiles, and many people from the country were crossing the bridge, he asked the meaning of this proceeding, and they told him these things. He said, "It is not meet to do this ignominy unto Daniel the prophet, but I command you to measure the bridge from both sides, and to take the coffin of Daniel and place it inside another coffin of crystal, so that the wooden coffin be within that of crystal, and to suspend this from the middle of the bridge by a chain of iron; at this spot you must build a synagogue for all comers, so that whoever wishes to pray there, be he Jew or Gentile, may do so." And to this very day the coffin is suspended from the bridge. And the king commanded that out of respect for Daniel no fisherman should catch fish within a mile above or a mile below.

The reputed sepulcher of Daniel is situated between Schuster and Dizful in Persia, close by the river Shaour, an affluent of the Karun river, which is supposed to be the Ulai of the Bible, (Dan. viii. 2). It is within sight of the vast mound which denotes the site of Susa, the ancient Shushan. [Adler]

Rudbar   Thence it takes three days to Rudbar where there are about 20,000 Israelites, and among them are learned and rich men. But the Jews live there under great oppression. Thence it is two days Nihawand   to Nihawand, where there are 4,000 Israelites. Thence it is four Mulahid   days to the land of Mulahid. Here live a people who do not profess the Mohammedan religion, but live on high mountains, and worship the Old Man of the land of the Hashishim. And among them there are four communities of Israel who go forth with them in war-time. They are not under the rule of the king of Persia, but reside in the high mountains, and descend from these mountains to pillage and to capture booty, and then return to the mountains, and none can overcome them. There are learned men amongst the Jews of their land. These Jews are under the authority of the Head of the Captivity in Babylon. Thence it is five days Amadia   to Amadia where there are about 25,000 Israelites. This is the first of those communities that dwell in the mountains of Chafton, where there are more than 100 Jewish communities. Here is the Media   commencement of the land of Media. These Jews belong to the first captivity which King Shalmanezar led away; and they speak the language in which the Targum is written. Amongst them are learned men. The communities reach from the province of Gilan   Amadia unto the province of Gilan, twenty-five days distant, on the border of the kingdom of Persia. They are under the authority of the king of Persia, and he raises a tribute from them through the hands of his officer, and the tribute which they pay every year by way of poll tax is one gold amir, which is equivalent to one and one-third maravedi. (This tax has to be paid by all males in the land of Islam who are over the age of fifteen.)

In Amadia there arose ten years ago, a man named David Alroy of the city of Amadia. He studied under Chisdai, the Head of the Captivity, and under the Head of the Academy, Gaon Jacob, in the city of Baghdad, and he was well versed in the Law of Israel, in the Halachah, as well as in the Talmud, and in all the wisdom of the Mohammedans; also in secular literature and in the writings of magicians and soothsayers. He conceived the idea of rebelling against the king of Persia, and of collecting the Jews who live in the mountains of Chafton to go forth and to fight against all the nations, and to march and capture Jerusalem. He showed signs by pretended miracles to the Jews, and said, "The Holy One, blessed be He, sent me to capture Jerusalem and to free you from the yoke of the Gentiles." And the Jews believed in him and called him their Messiah. When the king of Persia heard of it he sent for him to come and speak with him. Alroy went to him without fear, and when he had audience of the king, the latter asked him, "Art thou the king of the Jews?" He answered, "I am." Then the king, in great wrath, commanded that he should be seized and placed in the prison of the king, the place where the king's prisoners were bound unto the day of their death, in the city of Tabaristan which is on the large river Gozan.

At the end of three days, while the king was sitting deliberating with his princes concerning the Jews who had rebelled, David suddenly stood before them. He had escaped from the prison without the knowledge of any man. And when the king saw him, he said to him, "Who brought thee hither, and who has released thee?" "My own wisdom and skill," answered the other, "for I am not afraid of thee, nor of any of thy servants." The king forthwith loudly bade his servants to seize him, but they answered, "We cannot see any man, although our ears hear him." Then the king and all his princes marvelled at his subtlety; but he said to the king, "I will go my way;" so he went forth. And the king went after him; and the princes and servants followed their king until they came to the riverside. Then Alroy took off his mantle and spread it on the face of the water to cross thereon. When the servants of the king saw that he crossed the water on his mantle, they pursued him in small boats, wishing to bring him back, but they were unable, and they said, "There is no wizard like this in the whole world." That self-same day he went a journey of ten days to the city of Amadia by the strength of the ineffable Name, and he told the Jews all that had befallen him, and they were astonished at his wisdom.

After that the king of Persia sent word to the Emir Al-Mumi-nin, the Caliph of the Mohammedans at Baghdad, urging him to warn the Head of the Exile, and the Head of the Academy, Gaon Jacob, to restrain David Alroy from executing his designs. And he threatened that he would otherwise slay all the Jews in his Empire. Then all the congregations of the land of Persia were in great trouble. And the Head of the Captivity, and the Head of the Academy, Gaon Jacob, sent to Alroy, saying, "The time of redemption is not yet arrived; we have not yet seen the signs thereof; for by strength shall no man prevail. Now our mandate is, that thou cease from these designs, or thou shalt surely be ex-communicated from all Israel." And they sent unto Zakkai the Nasi, in the land of Assur (Mosul) and unto R. Joseph Burhan-al-mulk, the astronomer there, bidding them to send on the let-ter to Alroy, and furthermore they themselves wrote to him to warn him, but he would not accept the warning. Then there arose a king of the name of Sin-ed-din, the king of the Togarmim, and a vassal of the king of Persia, who sent to the father-in-law of David Alroy, and gave him a bribe of 10,000 gold pieces to slay Alroy in secret. So he went to Alroy's house, and slew him whilst he was asleep on his bed. Thus were his plans frustrated. Then the king of Persia went forth against the Jews that lived in the mountains; and they sent to the Head of the Captivity to come to their assistance and to appease the king. He was eventually appeased by a gift of 100 talents of gold, which they gave him, and the land was at peace thereafter.

David Alroy, being a young man of engaging appearance and great accomplishments, gained considerable influence with the governor of Amadia, and had a considerable following among the Jews of Persia. With the intention of occupying the castle, he introduced a number of his armed adherents into the town, who were careful, however, to conceal their weapons. The governor detected the conspiracy, and put Alroy to death. The excitement among the Jews lasted for a considerable time. Two imposters, with letters purporting to emanate from Alroy, came to Baghdad, and worked upon the credulity of the community. Men and women parted with their money and jewelry, having been brought to believe that on a certain night they would be able to fly on angels' wings from the roofs of their houses to Jerusalem. The only thing which made the women feel unhappy was the fear that their little ones might not be able to keep pace with them in the aerial flight. At daybreak the fraud was discovered, but the impostors had meanwhile decamped with their treasure. [Adler]

From this mountain it is a journey of twenty days to Hamadan, *Hamadan* which is the great city of Media, where there are 30,000 Israelites. In front of a certain synagogue, there are buried Mordecai and Esther.

Dr. J. E. Polak, formerly Physician to the late Shah of Persia, gives the desired information in an interesting work on Persia. He writes as follows: "The only national monument which the Jews in Persia possess is the tomb of Esther at Hamadan, the ancient Ecbatana, whither they have made pilgrimages from time immemorial. In the center of the Jewish quarter there is to be seen a low building with a cupola, on the top of which a stork has built its nest. The entrance is walled up for the greater part; there only remains below a small aperture which can be closed by a movable flat stone serving the purpose of a door and affording some protection from attacks, which are not uncommon. In the entrance hall, which has but a low ceiling, are recorded the names of pilgrims; also the year when the building was restored. Thence one gains access into a small four-cornered chamber in which there are two high sarcophagi made of oak, which are the monuments of Esther and Mordecai. On both of them are inscribed in Hebrew the words of the last chapter of the Book of Esther, as well as the names of three Physicians at whose expense the tomb was repaired." Dr. Polak states that in the Middle Ages the Jewish population of Persia was very large, especially in the southern provinces. In recent years it has greatly diminished in consequence of dire persecution. He was assured that not more than 2,000 Jewish families remained in the country. Eighty years ago the entire community at Meshed were forcibly converted to Islam. [Adler]

Tabaristan   From thence (Hamadan) it takes four days to Tabaristan, which is situated on the river Gozan. Some 4,000 Jews live there.
Isfahan   Thence it is seven days to Ispahan, the great city and the royal residence. It is twelve miles in circumference, and about 15,000 Israelites reside there. The Chief Rabbi is Sar Shalom, who has been appointed by the Head of the Captivity to have jurisdiction over all the Rabbis that are in the kingdom of Persia. Four days
Fars   onward is Shiraz, which is the city of Fars, and 10,000 Jews live
Ghaznah   there. Thence it is seven days to Ghaznah, the great city on the river Gozan, where there are about 80,000 Israelites. It is a city of commercial importance; people of all countries and tongues come thither with their wares. The land is extensive.
Samarkand   Thence it is five days to Samarkand, which is the great city on the confines of Persia. In it live some 50,000 Israelites, and R. Obadiah the Nasi, is their appointed head. Among them are wise and very rich men.
Tibet   Thence it is four days' journey to Tibet, the country in whose forests the musk is found.
Naisabur   Thence it takes twenty-eight days to the mountains of Naisabur by the river Gozan. And there are men of Israel in the land of Persia who say that in the mountains of Naisabur four of the tribes

of Israel dwell, namely, the tribe of Dan, the tribe of Zebulun, the tribe of Asher, and the tribe of Naphtali, who were included in the first captivity of Shalmaneser, king of Assyria, as it is written (2Kings xviii. 11): "And he put them in Halah and in Habor by the river of Gozan and in the cities of the Medes."

> We draw attention to the cautious manner in which Benjamin speaks here and elsewhere when alluding to the whereabouts of any of the ten tribes. The tradition is widespread that independent Jewish tribes were to be found in Khorasan until recent times. [Adler]

The extent of their land is twenty days' journey, and they have cities and large villages in the mountains; the river Gozan forms the boundary on the one side. They are not under the rule of the Gentiles, but they have a prince of their own, whose name is R. Joseph Amarkala the Levite. There are scholars among them. And they sow and reap and go forth to war as far as the land of Cush *Cush* by way of the desert.

> It should be remembered that *Cush* in ancient Jewish literature does not always signify Ethiopia, but also denotes parts of Arabia, especially those nearest to Abyssinia. The name *Cush* is also applied to countries east of the Tigris. [Adler]

They are in league with the Kofar-al-Turak, who worship the wind and live in the wilderness, and who do not eat bread, nor drink wine, but live on raw uncooked meat. They have no noses, and in lieu thereof they have two small holes, through which they breathe. They eat animals both clean and unclean, and they are very friendly towards the Israelites. Fifteen years ago they overran the country of Persia with a large army and took the city of Rayy; they smote it with the edge of the sword, took all the spoil thereof, and returned by way of the wilderness. Such an invasion had not been known in the land of Persia for many years. When the king of Persia heard thereof his anger was kindled against them, and he said, "Not in my days nor in the days of my fathers did an army sally forth from this wilderness. Now I will go and cut off their name from the earth." A proclamation was made throughout his Empire, and he assembled all his armies; and he sought a guide who might show him the way to their encampment. And a certain man said that he would show him the way, as he was one of them. And the king promised that he would enrich him if he did so. And the king asked him as to what provisions they would require for the march through the wilderness. And he replied, "Take with you bread and wine for fifteen days, for you will find no sustenance by the way, till you have reached their land." And they did so, and marched through the wilderness for fifteen days, but they found nothing at all. And their food began to give out, so that man and beast were dying of hunger and thirst. Then the king called to the guide, and said to him "Where is your promise to us that you would find our adversaries?" To which the other replied, "I have mistaken the way." And the king was wroth, and commanded that his head should be struck off. And the king further gave orders throughout the camp that every man who had any food should divide it with his neighbor. And they consumed everything they had, including their beasts. And after a further thirteen days' march they reached the mountains of Naisabur, where Jews lived. They came there on the Sabbath, and encamped in the gardens and plantations and by the springs of water which are by the side of the river Gozan. Now it was the time of the ripening of the fruit, and they ate and consumed everything. No man came forth to them, but on the mountains they saw cities and many towers. Then the king commanded two of his servants to go and inquire of the people who lived in the mountains, and to cross the river either in boats or by swimming. So they searched and found a large bridge, on which there were three towers, but the gate of the bridge was locked. And on the other side of the bridge was a great city. Then they shouted in front of the bridge till a man came forth and asked them what they wanted and who they were. But they did not understand him till an interpreter came who understood their language. And when he asked them, they said, "We are the servants of the king of Persia, and we have come to ask who you are, and whom you serve." To which the other replied: "We are Jews; we have no king and no Gentile prince, but a Jewish prince rules over us." They then questioned him with regard to the infidels, the sons of Ghuz of the Kofar-al-Turak, and he answered, "Truly they are in league with us, and he who seeks to do them harm seeks our harm." Then they went their way, and told the king of Persia, who was much alarmed. And on a certain day the Jews asked him to join combat with them, but he answered: "I am not come to fight you, but the Kofar-al-Turak, my enemy, and if you fight against me I will be avenged on you by killing all the Jews in my Empire; I know that you are stronger than I am in this place, and my army has come out of this great wilderness starving and athirst. Deal kindly with me and do not fight against me, but leave me to engage with the Kofar-al-Turak, my enemy, and sell me also the provisions which I require for my self and my army." The Jews then took counsel together, and resolved to propitiate the king on account of the Jews who were in exile in his Empire. Then the king entered their land with his army, and stayed there fifteen days. And they showed him much honour, and also sent a dispatch to the Kofar-al-Turak, their allies, reporting the matter to them. Thereupon the latter occupied the mountain passes in force with a large army composed of all those who dwelt in that desert, and when the king of Persia went forth to fight with them, they placed themselves in battle array against him. The Kofar-al-Turak army was victorious and slew many of the Persian host, and the king of Persia fled with only a few followers to his own country.

There can be little doubt that the Kofar-al-Turak, a people belonging to the Tartar stock, are identical with the so-called subjects of
Prester John, of whom so much was heard in the Middle Ages. They
defeated Sinjar in the year 1141; this was, however, more than fifteen years prior to Benjamin's visit. To judge from the above passage,
where the allies of the Jews are described as "infidels, the sons of Ghuz
of the Kofar-al-Turak," Benjamin seems to confound the Ghuzes
with the Tartar hordes. Now the Ghuzes belonged to the Seldjuk
clans who had become Mohammedans more than 100 years before,
and, as such, Benjamin would never have styled them infidels. These
Ghuzes waged war with Sinjar in 1153, when he was signally defeated,
and eventually made prisoner. It is to this battle that Benjamin must
have made reference, when he writes that it took place fifteen years
ago. [Adler]

Now a horseman, one of the servants of the king of Persia, en-
ticed a Jew, whose name was R. Moses, to come with him, and
when he came to the land of Persia this horseman made the Jew
his slave. One day the archers came before the king to give a
display of their skill and no one among them could be found to
draw the bow like this R. Moses. Then the king inquired of him
by means of an interpreter who knew his language, and he related
all that the horseman had done to him. Thereupon the king at
once granted him his liberty, had him clad in robes of silk, gave
him gifts, and said to him, "If thou wilt embrace our religion,
I will make thee a rich man and steward of my house," but he
answered, "My lord, I cannot do this thing." Then the king took
him and placed him in the house of the Chief Rabbi of the Ispahan
community, Sar Shalom, who gave him his daughter to wife.
This same R. Moses told me all these things.

Thence one returns to the land of Khuzistan which is by the
river Tigris, and one goes down the river which falls into the In-
Kish   dian Ocean unto an island called Kish. It is a six days' journey

to reach this island.[It should be noted here that Benjamin used Hebrew terms implying that he himself did not go to sea.]

In the Middle Ages the island of Kish or Kis was an important station on the trade route from India to Europe. In the course of the twelfth century it became the trade center of the Persian Gulf. A great walled city was built in the island, where water tanks had been constructed, and on the neighboring seabanks was the famous pearl fishery. Ships from India and Arabia crowded the port. Kish was afterwards supplanted by Ormuz and Bandar-Abbas. [Adler]

The inhabitants neither sow nor reap. They possess only one well, and there is no stream in the whole island, but they drink rain water. The merchants who come from India and the islands, encamp there with their wares. Moreover, men from Shinar, El-Yemen, and Persia bring thither all sorts of silk, purple, and flax, cotton, hemp, worked wool, wheat, barley, millet, rye, and all sorts of food, and lentils of every description, and they trade with one another, whilst the men from India bring great quantities of spices thither. The islanders act as middlemen, and earn their livelihood thereby. There are about 500 Jews there.

Thence it is ten days' journey by sea to Katifa, where there are about 5,000 Jews. Here the bdellium is to be found. On the twenty-fourth of Nisan rain falls upon the water, upon the surface of which certain small sea animals float, which drink in the rain and then shut themselves up, and sink to the bottom. And about the middle of Tishri men descend to the bed of the sea by ropes, and collect these shell-fish, then split them open and extract the pearls. This pearl fishery belongs to the king of the country, but is controlled by a Jewish official.

Katifa

Katifa or El-Katif lies on the Persian Gulf, on the East coast of Arabia, near Bahrein. Bochart is of opinion that this part of Arabia is the land of Havilah where, according to Gen. ii. 11 and 12, there is gold, bdellium, and the onyx stone. Jewish authorities are divided in opinion as to whether bdellium is a jewel, or the fragrant gum exuded by a species of balsam tree. Masudi is one of the earliest Arabic writers who gives us a description of the pearl fisheries in the Persian Gulf, and it very much accords with Benjamin's account. [Adler]

Khulam   Thence it is seven days' journey to Khulam which is the beginning of the country of the Sun-worshippers.

Khulam, now called Quilon, was a much frequented seaport in the early Middle Ages where Chinese shippers met the Arab traders. It afterwards declined in importance, being supplanted by Calicut, Goa, and eventually by Bombay. It was situated at the southern end of the coast of Malabar.

Under the heading "Cochin," the *Jewish Encyclopaedia* gives an account of the White and Black Jews of Malabar. By way of supplementing the article, it may be well to refer to a MS., of the Merzbacher Library formerly at Munich. From this MS. it appears that 10,000 exiled Jews reached Malabar A.C. 68 (i.e. about the time of the destruction of the Second Temple) and settled at Cranganor, Dschalor, Madri and Plota. [Adler]

These are the sons of Cush, who read the stars, and are all black in color. They are honest in commerce. When merchants come to them from distant lands and enter the harbor, three of the king's secretaries go down to them and record their names, and then bring them before the king, whereupon the king makes himself responsible even for their property which they leave in the open, unprotected. There is an official who sits in his office, and the owner of any lost property has only to describe it to him when he hands it back. This custom prevails in all that country. From Passover to New Year, that is all during the summer, no man can go out of his house because of the sun, for the heat in that country is intense, and from the third hour of the day onward, everybody remains in his house till the evening. Then they go forth and kindle lights in all the market places and all the streets, and then do their work and business at night-time. For they have to turn night into day in consequence of the great heat of the sun. Pepper is found there. They plant the trees thereof in the fields, and each man of the city knows his own plantation. The trees are small, and the pepper is as white as snow. And when they have collected it, they place it in saucepans and pour boiling water over it, so that it may become strong. They then take it out of the water and dry it in the sun, and it turns black. Calamus and ginger and many other kinds of spice are found in this land.

The people of this country do not bury their dead, but embalm them by means of various spices, after which they place them on chairs and cover them with fine linen. And each family has a house where it preserves the embalmed remains of its ancestors and relations. The flesh hardens on the bones, and the embalmed bodies look like living beings, so that every man can recognize his parents, and the members of his family for many years. They worship the sun, and they have high places everywhere outside the city at a distance of about half a mile. And every morning they run forth to greet the sun, for on every high place a solar disc is made of cunning workmanship and, as the sun rises, the disc rotates with thundering noise, and all, both men and women, offer incense to the sun with censers in their hands. Such are their superstitious practices. And throughout the island, including all the towns there, live several thousand Israelites. The inhabitants are all black, and the Jews are also. The latter are good and benevolent. They know the law of Moses and the prophets, and to a small extent the Talmud and Halacha.

Thence it is twenty-three days by sea to Ibrig/Ceylon, and the *Ceylon* inhabitants are fire worshippers, and are called Duchbin. Among them are about 3,000 Jews, and these Duchbin have priests in their several temples who are great wizards in all manner of witchcraft, and there are none like them in all the earth. In front of the high place of their temple there is a deep trench, where they keep a great fire alight all the year, and they call it Elahutha. And they cause their sons and daughters to pass through the fire, and even their dead they throw into it. Some of the great men of the country make a vow to die by fire. In such cases the man communicates his intention to the members of his household and his relations, and says:—"I have vowed to throw myself in the fire whilst I am yet alive." Then they answer, saying: "Happy art thou." And when the day of the performance of his vow arrives, they prepare for him a grand banquet, and if he is rich he rides on horseback, if poor he goes on foot to the border of the trench and throws himself into the fire. And all the members of his family shout to the accompaniment of timbrels and dancing until the body is entirely consumed. At the end of three days two of their high priests come to his house and to his children and say unto them: "Arrange the house, for this day your father will come to give his last directions as to what ye shall do." And they bring witnesses from the city. Then Satan is made to appear in the likeness of the deceased, and when his widow and children ask him how he fares in the other world he answers: "I went to my companions, but they would not receive me until I had discharged my obligations to the members of my house and to my neighbors." Then he makes his will and divides his property among his children, and gives directions that all his creditors should be paid and that his debts should be collected. Then the witnesses write out the will, and he goes his way and is seen no more. And by means of this trickery and witchcraft which these priests practice, the people are confirmed in their errors and assert that there is none in all the land like their priests.

Thence to cross over to the land of Zin (China) is a voyage of China forty days. Zin is in the uttermost East, and some say that there is the Sea of Nikpa (Ning-po?), where the star Orion predominates and stormy winds prevail.

Benjamin's statements as to India and China are of course very vague, but we must remember he was the first European who as much as mentions China. Having regard to the full descriptions of other countries of the old World by Arabic writers of the Middle Ages, and to the fact that the trade route then was principally by sea on the route indicated by Benjamin, it is surprising that we have comparatively little information about India and China from Arabic sources. In none of their records is the Sea of Nikpa named, and it is not improbable that Benjamin coined this name himself. [Adler]

At times the helmsman cannot govern his ship, as a fierce wind drives her into this Sea of Nikpa, where she cannot move from her place; and the crew have to remain where they are till their stores of food are exhausted and then they die. In this way many a ship has been lost, but men eventually discovered a device by which to escape from this evil place. The crew provide themselves with hides of oxen. And when this evil wind blows which drives them into the Sea of Nikpa, they wrap themselves up in the skins, which they make waterproof and, armed with knives, plunge into the sea. A great bird called the griffin spies them out, and in the belief that the sailor is an animal, the griffin seizes hold of him, brings him to dry land, and puts him down on a mountain or in a hollow in order to devour him. The man then quickly thrusts at the bird with a knife and slays him. Then the man issues forth from the skin and walks till he comes to an inhabited place. And in this manner many a man escapes.

Marco Polo has much to say about the bird "gryphon" when speaking of the sea currents which drive ships form Malabar to Madagascar.

He says: "It is for all the world like an eagle, but one indeed of enormous size. It is so strong that it will seize an elephant in its talons
and carry him high into the air and drop him so that he is smashed
to pieces; having so killed him, the gryphon swoops down on him
and eats him at leisure. The people of those isles call the bird 'Rukh.'"
Yule has an interesting note showing how old and widespread the
fable of the Rukh was, and is of the opinion that the reason that the
legend was localized in the direction of Madagascar was perhaps that
some remains of the great fossil Aepyornis and its colossal eggs were
found in that island. Professor Sayce states that the Rukh figures
much—not only in Chinese folklore—but also in the old Babylonian
literature. The bird is, of course, familiar to readers of *The Arabian
Nights*. [Adler]

Al-Gingaleh   Thence to Al-Gingaleh is a voyage of fifteen days, and about
Chulan   1,000 Israelites dwell there. Thence by sea to Chulan is seven days;
Zebid   but no Jews live there. From there it is twelve days to Zebid,
where there are a few Jews. From there it is eight days' journey
India   to India which is on the mainland, called the land of Aden, and
this is the Eden which is in Thelasar.

Neither Al-Gingaleh nor Chulan can be satisfactorily identified.
Benjamin has already made it clear that to get from India to China
takes sixty-three days, that is to say twenty-three days from Khulam
to Ibrig, and thence forty days to the sea of Nikpa. The return
journey, not merely to India but to Zebid, which Abulfeda and
Alberuni call the principal port of Yemen, seems to take but thirty-
four days. Ibn Batuta says about Aden: "It is situated on the seashore
and is a large city, but without either seed, water, or tree. They have
reservoirs in which they collect the rain for drinking. Some rich merchants reside here, and vessels from India occasionally arrive." A
Jewish community has been there from time immemorial. The men
until recent times used to go about all day in their Tephillin. [Adler]

The country is mountainous. There are many Israelites here, and
they are not under the yoke of the Gentiles, but possess cities and

castles on the summits of the mountains, from which they make descents into the plain country called Lybia, which is a Christian Empire. These are the Lybians of the land of Lybia, with whom the Jews are at war. The Jews take spoil and booty and retreat to the mountains, and no man can prevail against them. Many of these Jews of the land of Aden come to Persia and Egypt.

Lybia/ Abyssinia

> We must take Benjamin's statements here to mean that the independent Jews who lived in the mountainous country in the rear of Aden crossed the Straits of Bab-el-Mandeb and made war against the inhabitants of the Plains of Abyssinia. The Jews coming from Aden had to encounter the forces of the Christian sovereign of Abyssinia, and sought saftey in the mountainous regions of that country. Here they were heard of later under the name of Falasha Jews. [Adler]

To Africa

THENCE to the land of Assuan is a journey of twenty days through the desert. This is Seba on the river Pishon (Nile) which descends from the land of Cush. And some of these sons of Cush have a king whom they call the Sultan Al-Ha-bash. There is a people among them who, like animals, eat of the herbs that grow on the banks of the Nile and in the fields. They go about naked and have not the intelligence of ordinary men. They cohabit with their sisters and any one they find. The climate is very hot. When the men of Assuan make a raid into their land, they take with them bread and wheat, dry grapes and figs, and throw the food to these people, who run after it. Thus they bring many of them back prisoners, and sell them in the land of Egypt and in the surrounding countries. And these are the black slaves, the sons of Ham.

From Assuan it is a distance of twelve days to Heluan where there are about 300 Jews. Thence people travel in caravans a journey of fifty days through the great desert called Sahara, to the land of Zawilah, which is Havilah in the land of Gana. In this desert there are mountains of sand, and when the wind rises, it covers the caravans with the sand, and many die from suffocation. Those that escape bring back with them copper, wheat, fruit, all manner of lentils, and salt. And from thence they bring gold, and all kinds of jewels. This is in the land of Cush which is called Al-Habash on the western confines. From Heluan it is thirteen days' journey to Kutz which is Kūs, and this is the commencement of the land of Egypt. At Kutz there are 300 Jews. Thence it is 300 miles to Fayum, which is Pithom, where there are 200 Jews; and

Heluan

Sahara

Zawilah/ Gana

Kutz/ Egypt

Fayum

unto this very day one can see ruins of the buildings which our forefathers erected there.

Among the buildings, grain-stores have been discovered in the form of deep rectangular chambers without doors, into which the corn was poured from above. These are supposed to date from the time of Rameses II. The Fayum, or Marsh-district, owes its extraordinary fertility to the Bahr Yussuf (Joseph's Canal).

The Arab story is that when Joseph was getting old the courtiers tried to bring about his disgrace by inducing Pharaoh to set him what appeared to be an impossible task, viz. to double the revenues of the province within a few years. Joseph accomplished the task by artificially adapting a natural branch of the Nile so as to give the district the benefit of the yearly overflow. The canal thus formed, which is 207 miles in length, was called after Joseph. The storehouses of Joseph are repeatedly mentioned by Arabic writers. [Adler]

Mizraim/ Cairo

Thence to Mizraim is a journey of four days. This Mizraim is the great city situated on the banks of the Nile, which is Pison or Al-Nil. The number of Jewish inhabitants is about 7,000.

To comprehend fully Benjamin's account, we must remember that at the time of his visit the metropolis was passing through a crisis. Since March, 1169, Saladin had virtually become the ruler of Egypt, although nominally he acted as Vizier to the Caliph El-Adid, who was the last of the Fatimite line, and who died September 13, 1171, three days after his deposition. The well-known citadel of Cairo, standing on the spurs of the Mukattam Hills, was erected by Saladin seven years later. The Cairo of 1170, which was styled El Medina, was founded in 969, and consisted of an immense palace for the Caliph and his large household. It was surrounded by quarters for a large army, and edifices for the ministers and government offices. The whole was protected by massive walls and imposing Norman-like gates. The civil population—more particularly the Jews—dwelt in the old Kasr-esh-Shama quarter round the so-called Castle of

Babylon, also in the city of Fostat, founded in 641, and in the El-Askar quarter, which was built in 751. These suburbs went under the name of Misr or Masr, but are called by Benjamin "Mizraim." Fostat was set on fire on November 12, 1168, by the order of the Vizier Shawar, in order that it might not give shelter to the Franks who had invaded Egypt, but was soon rebuilt in part. It now goes under the name Masr-el-Atika, and is noted at the present day for its immense rubbish heaps. [Adler]

Two large synagogues are there, one belonging to the men of the land of Israel and one belonging to the men of the land of Babylon. The synagogue of the men of the land of Israel is called Kenisat-al-Schamiyyin, and the synagogue of the men of Babylon is called Kenisat-al-Irakiyyin. Their usage with regard to the portions and sections of the Law is not alike; for the men of Babylon are accustomed to read a portion every week, as is done in Spain, and is our custom, and to finish the Law each year; whilst the men of Palestine do not do so, but divide each portion into three sections and finish the Law at the end of three years. The two communities, however, have an established custom to unite and pray together on the day of the Rejoicing of the Law, and on the day of the Giving of the Law. Among the Jews is Nethanel, the Prince of Princes and the head of the Academy, who is the head of all the congregations in Egypt; he appoints Rabbis and officials, and is attached to the court of the great King, who lives in his palace of Zoan el-Medina, which is the royal city for the Arabs. Here resides the Emir al Muminin, a descendant of Abu Talib. All his subjects are called "Alawiyyim," because they rose up against the Emir al Muminin al Abbasi (the Abbaside Caliph) who resides at Baghdad. And between the two parties there is a lasting feud, for the former have set up a rival throne in Zoan (Egypt).

Twice in the year the Egyptian monarch goes forth, once on the occasion of the great festival, and again when the river Nile rises. Zoan is surrounded by a wall, but Mizraim has no wall, for the river encompasses it on one side. It is a great city, and it has market places as well as inns in great number. The Jews that dwell there are very rich. No rain falls, neither is ice or snow ever seen. The climate is very hot.

The river Nile rises once a year in the month of Elul [August-September]; it covers all the land, and irrigates it to a distance of fifteen days' journey. The waters remain upon the surface of the land during the months of Elul and Tishri, and irrigate and fertilize it.

The inhabitants have a pillar of marble, erected with much skill, in order to ascertain the extent of the rise of the Nile. It stands in the front of an island in the midst of the water, and is twelve cubits high. When the Nile rises and covers the column, they know that the river has risen and has covered the land for a distance of fifteen days' journey to its full extent. If only half the column is covered, the water only covers half the extent of the land. And day by day an officer takes a measurement on the column and makes proclamation thereof in Zoan and in the city of Mizraim, proclaiming: "Give praise unto the Creator, for the river this day has risen to such and such a height;" each day he takes the measurement and makes his proclamation. If the water covers the entire column, there will be abundance throughout Egypt. The river continues to rise gradually till it covers the land to the extent of fifteen days' journey. He who owns a field hires workmen, who dig deep trenches in his field, and fish come with the rise of the water and enter the trenches. Then, when the waters have receded, the fish remain behind in the trenches, and the owners of the fields take them and either eat them or sell them to the fishmongers, who salt them and deal in them in every place. These fish are exceedingly fat and large, and the oil obtained from them is used in this land for lamp oil. Though a man eat a great quantity of these fish, if he but drink Nile water afterwards they will not hurt him, for the waters have medicinal properties. People ask, what causes the Nile to rise? The Egyptians say that up the river, in the land of Al-Habash (Abyssinia), which is the land of Havilah, much rain descends at the time of the rising of the river, and that this abundance of rain causes the river to rise and to cover the surface of the land. If the river does not rise, there is no sowing, and famine is sore in the land. Sowing is done in the month of Marheshvan, after the river has gone back to its ordinary channel. In the month of Adar [February-March] is the barley harvest, and in the month of Nisan [March-April] the wheat harvest.

In the month of Nisan they have cherries, pears, cucumbers, and gourds in plenty; also beans, peas, chickpeas, and many kinds of vegetables, such as purslane, asparagus, pulse, lettuce, coriander, endive, cabbage, leek, and cardoon. The land is full of all good things, and the gardens and plantations are watered from the various reservoirs and by the river water.

The river Nile, after flowing past (the city of) Mizraim, divides into four heads: one channel proceeds in the direction of Damietta, which is Caphtor, where it falls into the sea. The second channel flows to the city of Reshid (Rosetta), which is near Alexan- *Rosetta* dria, and there falls into the sea. The third channel goes by way of Ashmun, where it falls into the sea; and the fourth channel goes as far as the frontier of Egypt. Along both banks of these four river-heads are cities, towns, and villages, and people visit these places either by ship or by land. There is no such thickly populated land as this elsewhere. It is extensive too and abundant in all good things.

From New Mizraim unto Old Mizraim is a distance of two parasangs. The latter is in ruins, and the place where walls and houses stood can be seen to the present day. The store-houses also of Joseph, of blessed memory, are to be found in great numbers in many places. They are built of lime and stone, and are exceedingly strong. A pillar is there of marvellous workmanship, the like of which cannot be seen throughout the world.

Outside the city is the ancient synagogue of Moses our master, of blessed memory, and the overseer and clerk of this place of worship is a venerable old man; he is a man of learning, and they call him Al Sheik Abu al-Nazr. The extent of Mizraim, which is in ruins, is three miles.

Goshen/   Thence to the land of Goshen is eight parasangs—here is
Bilbais   Bilbais. There are about 300 Jews in the city, which is a large one. Thence it is half a day's journey to Ain-al-Shams or Ramses, which is in ruins. Traces are there to be seen of the buildings which our forefathers raised, namely, towers built of bricks. From
Al Bubizig   here it is a day's journey to Al Bubizig, where there are about 200
Benha   Jews. Thence it is half a day to Benha, where there are about 60
Muneh Sifte   Jews. Thence it takes half a day to Muneh Sifte, where there are
Samnu   500 Jews. From there it is half a day's journey to Samnu, where there are about 200 Jews. From there it is four parasangs to
Damira   Damira, where there are about 700 Jews. From there it is five days
Lammanah   to Lammanah where there are about 500 Jews.

Alexandria   Two days' journey takes one to Alexandria of Egypt, which is Ammon of No; but when Alexander of Macedon built the city he called it after his own name, and made it exceedingly strong and beautiful. The houses, the palaces, and the walls are of excellent architecture. Outside the town is the academy of Aristotle, the teacher of Alexander. This is a large building, standing between other academies to the number of twenty, with a column of marble between each. People from the whole world were wont to come hither in order to study the wisdom of Aristotle the philosopher. The city is built over a hollow by means of arches. Alexander built it with great understanding. The streets are wide and straight, so that a man can look along them for a mile from gate to gate, from the gate of Reshid to the gate by the sea.

Alexander also built for the harbor of Alexandria a pier, a king's highway running into the midst of the sea. And there he erected a large tower, a lighthouse, called Manar al Iskandriyyah in Arabic. On the top of the tower there is a glass mirror. Any ships that attempted to attack or molest the city, coming from Greece or from the Western lands, could be seen by means of this mirror of glass at a distance of twenty days' journey, and the inhabitants could thereupon put themselves on their guard. It happened once, many years after the death of Alexander, that a ship came from the land of Greece, and the name of the captain was Theodoros, a Greek of great cleverness. The Greeks at that time were under the yoke of Egypt. The captain brought great gifts in silver and gold and garments of silk to the King of Egypt, and he moored his ship in front of the lighthouse, as was the custom of all merchants.

Every day the guardian of the lighthouse and his servants had their meals with him, until the captain came to be on such friendly terms with the keeper that he could go in and out at all times. And one day he gave a banquet, and caused the keeper and all his servants to drink a great deal of wine. When they were all asleep, the captain and his servants arose and broke the mirror and departed that very night. From that day onward the Christians began to come thither with boats and large ships, and eventually captured the large island called Crete and also Cyprus, which are under the dominion of the Greeks. Ever since then, the men of the King of Egypt have been unable to prevail over the Greeks. To this day the lighthouse is a landmark to all seafarers who come to Alexandria; for one can see it at a distance of 100 miles by day, and at night the keeper lights a torch which the mariners can see from a distance, and thus sail towards it.

Josephus, who had the opportunity of seeing the Pharos before it was destroyed, must likewise have exaggerated when he said that the lighthouse threw its rays a distance of 300 stadia. Strabo describes the Pharos of Alexandria, which was considered one of the wonders of the world. As the coast was low and there were no landmarks, it proved of great service to the city. It was built of white marble, and on the top there blazed a huge beacon of logs saturated with pitch. Abulfeda alludes to the large mirror which enabled the lighthouse keepers to detect from a great distance the approach of the enemy. He further mentions that the trick by which the mirror was destroyed took place in the first century of Islamism, under the Caliph Valyd, the son of Abd-almalek. [Adler]

Alexandria is a commerical market for all nations. Merchants come thither from all the Christian kingdoms. On the one side, from the land of Venetia and Lombardy, Tuscany, Apulia, Amalfi, Sicilia, Calabria, Romagna, Khazaria, Patzinakia, Hungaria, Bulgaria, Rakuvia (Ragusa?), Croatia, Slavonia, Russia, Alamannia (Germany), Saxony, Danemark, Kurland? Ireland? Norway (Norge?), Frisia, Scotia, Angleterre, Wales, Flanders, Hainault? Normandy, France, Poitiers, Anjou, Burgundy, Maurienne, Provence, Genoa, Pisa, Gascony, Aragon, and Navarra. And towards the west, under the sway of the Mohammedans: Andalusia, Algarve, Africa, and the land of the Arabs. And on the other side India, Zawilah, Abyssinia, Lybia, El-Yemen, Shinar, Esh-Sham (Syria); also Javan, whose people are called the Greeks, and the Turks. And merchants of India bring thither all kinds of spices, and the merchants of Edom buy of them. And the city is a busy one and full of traffic. Each nation has an inn of its own.

By the seacoast there is a sepulcher of marble on which are engraved all manner of beasts and birds; an effigy is in the midst thereof, and all the writing is in ancient characters, which no one knows now. Men suppose that it is the sepulcher of a king who lived in early times before the Deluge. The length of the sepulcher is fifteen spans, and its breadth is six spans. There are about 3,000 Jews in Alexandria.

Thence it is two days' journey to Damietta, which is Caphtor, *Damietta*
where there are about 200 Jews, and it lies upon the sea. Thence
it is one day's journey to Simasim; it contains about 100 Jews. *Simasim*
From there it is half a day to Sunbat; the inhabitants sow flax and *Sunbat*
weave linen, which they export to all parts of the world. Thence
it is four days to Ailam, which is Elim. It belongs to the Arabs *Ailan*
who dwell in the wilderness. Thence it is two days' journey to
Rephidim where the Arabs dwell, but there are no Jews there. *Rephidim*
A day's journey from thence takes one to Mount Sinai. On top *Mt. Sinai*
of the mountain is a large convent belonging to the great monks,
called Syrians.

> The monastery of St. Catherine was erected 2,000 feet below the
> summit of Jebel Musa. It was founded by Justinian to give shelter
> to the numerous Syrian hermits who inhabited the peninsula. The
> monastery was presided over by an Archbishop. [Adler]

At the foot of the mountain is a large town called Tur Sinai; the
inhabitants speak the language of the Targum (Syriac). It is close
to a small mountain, five days distant from Egypt. The inhabitants are under Egyptian rule. At a day's journey from Mount
Sinai is the Red Sea, which is an arm of the Indian Ocean. We
return to Damietta. From there it is a day's journey to Tanis, *Tanis*
which is Hanes, where there are about 40 Jews. It is an island in
the midst of the sea. Thus far extends the empire of Egypt.

Return to Europe

HENCE it takes twenty days by sea to Messina, Messina/ which is the commencement of Sicily and is Sicily situated on the arm of the sea that is called Lipar, which divides it from Calabria. Here about 200 Calabria Jews dwell. It is a land full of everything good, with gardens and plantations. Here most of the pilgrims assemble to cross over to Jerusalem, as this is the best crossing. Thence it is about two days' journey to Palermo, which is a large city. Palermo here is the palace of King William. Palermo contains about 1,500 Jews and a large number of Christians and Mohammedans. It is in a district abounding in springs and brooks of water, a land of wheat and barley, likewise of gardens and plantations, and there is not the like thereof in the whole island of Sicily. Here is the domain and garden of the king, which is called Al Harbina (Al Hacina), containing all sorts of fruit trees. And in it is a large fountain. The garden is encompassed by a wall. And a reservoir has been made there which is called Al Buheira, and in it are many sorts of fish. Ships overlaid with silver and gold are there, belonging to the king, who takes pleasure trips in them with his women.

> King William II, surnamed "the Good," was sixteen years old when Benjamin visited Sicily in 1170. During the king's minority the Archbishop was the vice-regent. He was expelled in 1169 on account of his unpopularity. Chroniclers tell that when the young king was freed from the control of the viceroy he gave himself up to pleasure and dissipation. [Adler]

In the park there is also a great palace, the walls of which are painted, and overlaid with gold and silver; the paving of the floors is of marble, picked out in gold and silver in all manner of designs. There is no building like this anywhere. And this island, the commencement of which is Messina, contains all the pleasant things of this world. It embraces Syracuse, Marsala, Catania, Petralia, and Trapani—the circumference of the island being six days' journey. In Trapani coral is found, which is called Al Murgan.

> Edrisi, who wrote his Geography in Sicily in 1154 at the request of King Roger II, calls the island a pearl, and cannot find words sufficient in praise of its climate, beauty, and fertility. He is especially enthusiastic concerning Palermo. Petralia is described by him as being a fortified place, and an excellent place of refuge, the surrounding country being under a high state of cultivation and very productive. [Adler]

Thence people pass to the city of Rome in ten days. And from Rome they proceed by land to Lucca, which is a five days' journey. Thence they cross the mountain of Jean de Maurienne, and the passes of Italy. It is twenty days' journey to Verdun, which is the commencement of Alamannia [Germany], a land of mountains and hills. All the congregations of Alamannia are situated on the great river Rhine, from the city of Cologne, which is the principal town of the Empire, to the city of Regensburg, a distance of fifteen days' journey at the other extremity of Alamannia, otherwise called Ashkenaz. And the following are the cities in the land of Alamannia, which have Hebrew congregations: Metz, Treves on the river Moselle, Coblenz, Andernach, Bonn, Cologne, Bingen, Münster, and Worms.

Germany

All Israel is dispersed in every land, and he who does not further the gathering of Israel will not meet with happiness nor live with Israel. When the Lord will remember us in our exile, and raise the horn of his anointed, then every one will say, "I will lead the Jews and I will gather them." As for the towns which have been mentioned, they contain scholars and communities that love their brethren, and speak peace to those that are near and afar, and when a wayfarer comes they rejoice, and make a feast for him, and say, "Rejoice, brethren, for the help of the Lord comes in the twinkling of an eye." If we were not afraid that the appointed time has not yet arrived nor been reached, we would have gathered together, but we dare not do so until the time for song has arrived, and the voice of the turtle-dove (is heard in the land), when the messengers will come and say continually, "The Lord be exalted."

Meanwhile, they send missives one to the other, saying, "Be ye strong in the law of Moses, and do ye mourners for Zion and ye mourners for Jerusalem entreat the Lord, and may the supplication of those that wear the garments of mourning be received through their merits."

In addition to the several cities which we have mentioned there are besides: Strassburg, Würzburg, Mantern, Bamberg, Freising, and Regensburg at the extremity of the Empire. In these cities there are many Israelites, wise men and rich.

Thence extends the land of Bohemia, called Prague. This is the Bohemia/ commencement of the land of Slavonia, and the Jews who dwell Prague there call it Canaan, because the men of that land (the Slavs) sell their sons and their daughters to the other nations. These are the men of Russia, which is a great empire stretching from the gates of Prague to the gates of Kieff, the large city which is at the ex- Russia/ tremity of that empire. It is a land of mountains and forests, where Kiev there are to be found the animals called vair [marten], ermine, and sable. No one issues forth from his house in wintertime on account of the cold. People are to be found there who have lost the tips of their noses by reason of the frost. Thus far reaches the empire of Russia.

France/   The kingdom of France, which is Zarfath, extends from the
Paris   town of Auxerre unto Paris, the great city—a journey of six days.
The city belongs to King Louis. It is situated on the river Seine.
Scholars are there, unequalled in the whole world, who study the
Law day and night. They are charitable and hospitable to all
travellers, and are as brothers and friends unto all their brethren,
the Jews. May God, the Blessed One, have mercy upon us and
upon them!

[FINISHED AND COMPLETED]

NOTES TO BENJAMIN

Sepharad: The Hebrew name which refers to the Iberian Peninsula or Spain. The name is mentioned in the book of Obadiah
v. 20.

parasang: A Persian measure of length, usually reckoned as equal
to between three and three and one-half English miles.

Arukh: A lexicon and dictionary of all the words of Talmudic
literature, alphabetically arranged, written by Nathan ben
Yehiel of Rome (1020–1106).

Nathan the Expounder: An Expounder (*Darshan*) is the title given
to a writer of homilies on Scripture. These homilies were
delivered in the synagogues on the Sabbath. It was not a paid
position.

Aphilon: (Achelous) The river Achelous falls into the Ionian Sea
opposite Ithaca. [Adler]
Anatolica: Now known as Aetolicum. [Adler]

Warden: A communal leader usually associated with the distribution of *Tzedaqa*, or communal charitable funds; *Parnas* in
Hebrew.

Leading Man: The head of the congregation; in some medieval Jewish communities the "leading man" or *Rosh* was the chief officer of the community who was responsible for affixing his signature to legal documents.

PAGE 70

Shinar: A biblical name for Mesopotamia.

Khazars: A Turkic group which settled in the region of the Volga and the Don rivers sometime in the fifth century. The Khazars played an important role in Byzantine and Islamic politics because of their strategic location which bridged the two empires. There is evidence that in the mid-eighth century the leadership of the Khazars professed Judaism. We do not have precise knowledge of the nature of their Jewish religion. Benjamin would have know about the correspondence between the Khazars and the tenth-century Spanish Jewish leader Hisdai Ibn Shaprut, as well as from his own travels.

Petachya [Pethachia] of Regensburg: A twelfth-century traveller who passed through Poland, Russia, Crimea, Khazaria, Armenia, Kurdistan, and Israel. He began his journey in 1175. The record of his travels seems to have been a summary of a longer narrative. Petachya's travels reflect the more pietistic atmosphere of Northern Europe. His aim appears to have been pilgrimage to the graves of Jewish holy men. Like Benjamin he was most impressed with the wealth and power of the Babylonian Jews.

PAGE 72

Karaïtes: Jews who rejected the rabbinic writings of the Talmud as authoritative and rooted their religious practice exclusively in Scripture *(Miqra)*. Karaism spread from Mesopotamia to Palestine and the Near East through the Balkans. Karaite groups continue to exist in the State of Israel.

PAGE 73

Mastic: A gum or resin which exudes from the bark of a tree; an item mentioned in commercial documents of Mediterranian traders during the middle ages.

PAGE 75

Epikursin: A Greek loan-word in Hebrew, which became a generic term, to designate any individual who deviated from rabbinic practice or theology.

PAGE 78

Druses: The information we possess of the history and religion of the Druses leads us to believe that they were emanations of the great schism of the Ismaelites, and that their religious tenets differed but little. The Druses still occupy the chain of Lebanon, and the residence of their emir is in the vicinity of Beirut, where R. Benjamin found them; and the atrocities committed by them very recently in the marauding expeditions which they undertook in 1838 and 1839 are a proof that their habits have not much changed since our author's time. [Adler]

Druses continue to live in Syria, Lebanon, and in Israel. They have a unique relationship with the government of Israel, and have had membership in the Israeli parliament.

PAGE 89

Rabbenu Hakadosh: "Our Holy Rabbi" refers to Rabbi Judah the Prince, who held the status of Patriarch of the Jewish community in the third century C.E. Rabbi Judah is the compiler of the *Mishnah*, the rabbinic compendium of the Oral Law.

Head of the Academy: *Rosh Yeshivah* carried with it the responsibility for the religious leadership of the Jewish communities in the land of Israel. Since this office was said to have evolved from the earlier Patriarchate of Palestine there were tensions between the Heads of the Academy in Babylonia and the Head of the Academy in the Land of Israel. In his description of Cairo, Benjamin will allude to the divided loyalties of the community to the two academies.

Beth Din: The chief religious court. These courts adjudicated both civil and religious laws.

Fifth of the Academy: This individual was the fifth in succession to the head of the academy.

Lecturer, Head of the Order: Honorific titles which indicate that the individual was at the same time a preacher and the master of studies in the academy.

Crown of Scholars: Honorific title for a master in the academy.

Nasi: Members of the families, ascribing their descent from King David, of the Head of the Exile, utilized the title *Nasi* or Prince. Recent research demonstrates that individuals titled "Nasi" appeared throughout the Islamic world during the Middle Ages, and furthered their personal ambitions by virtue of this title.

Gaon Jacob: The title of the heads of the Babylonian academies of Sura and Pumpeditha was *Rosh Yeshivah Gaon Jacob*, the

Head of the Academy, Pride of Jacob. The *Gaonim* were the highest authorities within the Jewry under the Caliph. They possessed power to adjudicate cases and to appoint judges for communities in the wide-spread Islamic empire. Each *Gaon* held authority over a large administrative district. Through pastoral letters and through the encouragement of questions of ritual nature, the *Gaonim* provided for the material sustenance of their academies. *Gaonim* were not elected, but appointed through an elaborate form of succession. Benjamin alludes to the formula for succession as he mentions the "second" or "fifth" in this passage. The honorific titles given to members of the Babylonian Gaonic families are analogous to the Palestine Gaon mentioned above.

PAGE 99

Batlanim: The Hebrew term literally means, "those who are idle." Benjamin uses the term here in a more specific context of scholars who have no material occupations and spend their time devoted to study of the sacred books of the Talmud. The *Batlanim* mentioned here may be Benjamin's method of describing Baghdad as a great city since it fulfills the rabbinic dictum, "What is a 'great city?' Any city which sustains ten *batlanim*."

Head of the Captivity: The chief sovereign of the Jewish community under the Caliphate. The Head of the Captivity was a descendant of the family of King David which was transferred to Mesopotamia during the Babylonian subjugation of the biblical kingdom of Judah. Under the Caliphate, he was responsible for the administration of the taxation of all Jewish communities in the empire. Benjamin's lengthy description of the power of the Exilarch indicates that the symbolism of the Davidic family remained important to the Jewish communities long after the Abbasid empire broke up into smaller kingdoms. The utilization of the verse from Genesis 49:10 "The scepter shall not depart from Judah, nor the ruler's staff from between his feet" is an indication of Benjamin's strong commitment to presenting Jewish sovereignty as a reality contemporary in the world of his reader.

PAGE 106

Mourners of Zion: An ascetic group which practiced rites of physical mortification and abstention in order to draw attention to the continuing exile of the Jewish people. These mourners are mentioned again by Benjamin as being found in communities of Arabia.

PAGE 107

Khaibar: In reading through the account, it is clear that Benjamin never visited the country, nor did he pretend to do so. [Adler]

Shalmaneser: King of Assyria (858–824 B.C.E.) who subjugated the Northern Kingdom of Israel and forced its King, Jehu, to pay tribute.

PAGE 110

Targum: Refers to the Aramaic translations of the Pentateuch and Prophets. These "translations" were considered sacred by medieval Jews. The people to whom Benjamin refers spoke an Aramaic or Syriac dialect. Jews in Kurdistan, until the modern period, continued to speak Aramaic.

PAGE 114

Naisabur: Naisabur is a city near Meshed and close to high mountains which are a continuation of the Elburz mountain range of Persia. [Adler]

Kofar-al-Turak: There can be little doubt that the Kofar-al-Turak, a people belonging to the Tartar stock are identical with the so-called subjects of Prester John, of whom so much was heard in the Middle Ages. They defeated Sinjar in the year 1141; this was, however, more than fifteen years prior to Benjamin's visit. To judge from the above passage, where the allies of the Jews are described as "infidels, the sons of Ghuz of the Kofar-al-Turak," Benjamin seems to confound the Ghuzes with the Tatar hordes. Now the Ghuzes belonged to the Seldjuk (Turk) clans who had become Mohammedans more than one hundred years before, and, as such, Benjamin would never have styled them as infidels. [Adler]

Nisan: The first month of the Hebrew calendar corresponding to the Spring months of March/April.

Sun-Worshippers: There is no doubt that Malabar became the asylum of this ancient sect, after it had been vanquished by the Mohammedans and had been forced by persecution, not only to seek refuge in the mountainous and less accessible parts of Persia, but to toil on to distant regions. They found a resting place, beyond the Indus, which they crossed in fear of the unrelenting pursuers, and here we still find their descendants, the Parsees. [Adler]

Kurland (?): Adler and Asher have divergent manuscript readings and translations for these geographic names. Many of them appear to be pure conjecture by the translators.

PAGE 138

Maurienne: At our author's time the Earldom of Maurienne included almost all of modern Savoy. We find a Count of Maurienne and Turin in the list of the noblemen who took part in the Second Crusade, and the name, which originated from the invasion of the Arabs in the ninth century is still retained in that of St. John Maurienne, a town at the foot of Mount Cenis. [Adler]

PAGE 140

King Louis: King Louis VII was King of France, 1137–1180.

Additional Notes of Clarification of Terms

Academy: The medieval Jewish Academy combined both the functions of teaching and judiciary. Young Jews would come to learn Talmud. A body of scholars also constituted a *Yeshivah* or Academy, which would render decisions on questions of Jewish practice.

Ammonites: Refers to peoples on the East Bank of the Jordan River. The Ammonites were defeated by both King Saul and King David.

Elul/Tishri: The sixth and seventh month of the Hebrew calendar corresponding to August/September of the Roman calendar. These two months are usually associated with repentance and preparation for the High Holy Days of Rosh HaShanah (New Year) and Yom Kippur (Day of Atonement).

Halacha: Literally, "the path" which Jews are bidden by God to walk in the ways of the divine commandments. Halacha refers to Jewish legal literature.

Jacobites: Members of a Christian group which rejected the Orthodox teaching that Christ had both a human and a divine nature. Jacobites believed that there was only a divine nature within the human Jesus Christ. The Jacobites became the national church of Syria before the Islamic conquest.

Jean-Phillipe Baratier, 1721–1735: French translator of Benjamin's travels. His translation appeared in 1734 in Amsterdam. The translation and notes written by Baratier denigrate the authenticity of Benjamin's work, as criticized by Asher in his bibliography.

Levite: A descendant of the biblical tribe of Levi. Traditional Jews who trace their descent from the Levitical tribe are entitled to special honors when they are called up to bless the scroll of the Torah during synagogue services. They also assist the *Kohanim* (those who trace their descent from Aaron, the high priest) during the blessing of the people on Jewish festivals.

Nestorian: A heterodox church which was persecuted in Syria and moved to Persian territory in the fifth century. They were well treated both by Persians and later by the Moslems. Although they were given the same status as Jews and Zoroastrians under Islamic law, they were subject to sporadic persecution.

Ninth of Ab: The date in the Hebrew calendar which is associated with the destruction of the Temple in Jerusalem by the Babylonians in 586 B.C.E., and by the Romans in 70 C.E. The Ninth of Ab became the focus for all subsequent tragedies in Jewish life, such as the Exile from Spain in 1492. In modern times Jews continue to mark the day with fasting and special poems of lamentation.

Tephillin: A small, leather case containing vellum strips inscribed with four passages from the Pentateuch (Ex. 13:1–10; Ex. 13:11–16; Deut. 6:4–9; Deut. 11:13–21). They have been worn in prayer by Jews from pre-Christian times, on the forehead and arm, on all days except the Sabbath and certain festivals, to remind them to keep the commandments.

ASHER BIBLIOGRAPHY

The Itinerary of Benjamin of Tudela: A Listing by
A. Asher

THE PRESENT WORK, though well known to the learned of the 13th, 14th and 15th centuries, was not printed before the year 1543, when the first edition appeared at Constantinople. Numerous reprints were called for in the course of time, of which the following is a catalogue.

I. EDITIONS IN HEBREW ONLY

I.   מסעות של רבי בנימן ·

Constantinople, Soncino 1543, in 8vo. 64 pages, printed in the rabbinic character.

This, the first edition, is so extremely rare, that notwithstanding the most diligent search, I have not been able to meet with any complete copy. It has been in the "Bibliothèque Royale" at Paris, but upon my inquiries after it—inquiries which met with the kindest attention—it could nowhere be found! The Oppenheim division of the Bodleian library contains an incomplete copy of this rare book, being deficient of the first fourteen pages, or one quarter of the whole work. In consequence of this unfortunate circumstance, I have not been able to report the title as fully as I ought to have done, according to the rules of bibliography. Like most other Hebrew books, which issued from the early Constantinople presses, this is but a very poor specimen of correctness and typography. All the mistakes of this "Princeps" have unfortunately crept into the editions noticed below in Nos. 3, 4, and 10, and have led the translators into error. The rarity constitutes the only value of this edition.

2.   מסעות על רבי בנימן ז׳׳ל . נדפס פה פיררא
בבית כ׳׳ד אברהם ן׳ אושקו יצ׳׳ו . שנת שי׳׳ו נחים .

Travels of R. Benjamin of blessed memory, printed at Ferrara in
the house of Abraham Ben Usque in the year 316 (1556), small 8vo.
64 pages, in the rabbinic character.

On the title is a globe in a square, surrounded by Hebrew
verses; the preface is on the verso of the title.

This second edition is perhaps rarer still than the first, and having evidently been printed from another M.S., is indispensably
necessary for a critique of the work. The text is much purer than
that of the former, and in many instances its readings give a sense,
where the former is too corrupt to be understood.

Unfortunately this edition was unknown to the early translators, B. Arias Montanus and L'Empereur, who would have
made less mistakes and formed a more correct judgment of our
author, had they been able to compare it with that of Constantinople. It forms the groundwork of the present edition and translation. No public library in France or Germany, most of which
I have personally visited or inquired at by correspondence, possesses a copy and the only one now known to exist is in the Oppenheim division of the Bodleian library at Oxford.

3.   מסעות של רבי בנימן . נדפס במדינת בריסגוייא
שנת שמ׳׳ג לפ׳׳ק על ידי הזיפרוני יצ ו .

Travels, etc. Printed in the country of Brisgau in the year 343
(1583) by the Siphroni, small 8vo. 32 pages, in the square character.

This is a reprint of the first (Constantinople) edition, it repeats
faithfully all the mistakes of that "Princeps" and has been altered
in those passages, where in speaking of Christians the former reads
התועים "the misled" into הנוצרים the "Nazarenes" probably
because it was revised by Christian censors. Some of the copies

appear to bear the imprint "Friburg in Brisgau," for thus do we find it quoted by different authors. (Wolff Biblioth. Hebr. vols I and III, N. 395.—Rodriguez de Castro. Biblioteca de los escritores Rabbinos españoles etc. p. 80) and it is almost certain the L'Empereur reprinted his edition from this, which is still preserved in the library of Leyden. All the books printed in Brisgau are rare, this is one of the rarest.—See a letter of thanks from Scaliger to Buxtorff for a copy of this edition in *Institut. Epist. Hebr.*, which although dated 1606, within about twenty years after its appearance, mentions the book as one of great rarity.

4.   מסעות של רבי בנימן ז"ל ·

Itinerarium D. Benjaminis Fr. M. Lugduni Batavorum apud Elzivirios. 1633. 24mo. 203pp. square character.

This edition was probably reprinted from that of Friburg (see above) and formed (as well as that quoted later in No. 13) part of the "*Respublicae Elzevirianae*," a collection well known to the amateurs of those "*Bijoux*" of the celebrated Dutch printers. Constantin L'Empereur, the learned editor, changed but very few words in the text and reserved his emendations for the notes, with which the edition quoted under No. 10 is enriched.

5.   מסעות של רבי בנימן הרופא ז"ל שנסע בג' חלקי
העולם: אירופא, אזיאה, אפריקא · ראה זה דבר חדש
אשר כבר היה לעולמים ונדפס שלש פעמים ומן השלשה
הכי נכבד · באשר שהראשונים הם בקצת מקומות
כספר חתום שקוראים מקומות ואינם יודעים מה הם
קוראים ונחת אין להם וכאן אתה מוצא כל דבר וכל
מקום על שם מכונו כמורגל בפי ההמוני והביאו לדפוס
התורני רבי אליקים בה"רר יעקב ש"ץ ז"ל חזן באמשטרדם
נדפס באמשטרדם אי"ע · בשנת נֹחַת לוה ומוה לפ"ק ·
בבית קשפר שטען ·

The Travels of Rabbi Benjamin the Physician (!) of blessed memory, who travelled in three parts of the world: in Europe, in Asia, and in Africa. See this new performance of a thing, that has been before, and has been printed three times, and of all the three this is the most preferable, in as far as the first (editions) are in many instances like a sealed book—for in most instances the names of the places mentioned are not known, and the perusal of the book therefore is without pleasure, and here thou wilt find each thing and each place under its present common name and acceptation. Printed at Amsterdam in the year 458 (1698) in the house of Caspar Sten. 24mo. 65 pages.

This edition was printed together with the *"Hope of Israel"* by R. Manasseh Ben Israel—the celebrated Rabbi, who exerted himself with Cromwell for the readmission of the Jews into England—and its pretended ameliorations are worse than useless. It is true the editor has translated many difficult Hebrew words into Jewish-German, but this labour is without any value, as it is founded not upon any critique but upon mere suggestion, and at best upon the translations of Arias Montanus and L'Empereur, which being in Latin, were very often misunderstood by the ignorant editor. The typography however is a beautiful specimen of the Dutch press.

6.

Travels etc. s. l. 1734.   מסעות וכו'

This edition, which I have not seen, is quoted by Dr. Zunz in *"Zeitschrift für die Wissenschaft des Judenthums."* Berlin 1823. p. 130.

7.   מסעות של רבי בנימן ; נדפסו בעיון יוחנן אנדריאס
מיכאל נאגיל לתועלת תלמידיו פה ישיבה מהוללה .
אלטדורף בשנת אתשס"ב בבית מדפים מהיר ומשובח
יוחנן אדם היוזיל .

Travels of R. Benjamin. Printed under the direction of John Andrew Michael Nagel, for the use of his scholars at this celebrated university. Altdorf 1762, printed by John Adam Hessel, small 8vo. 56 pp. square character.

A correct reprint of No. 4. of this list, containing even every mistake of its original. The editor, Nagel, has published fourteen dissertations on our author, and this edition of the "Travels" is so rare that Meusel doubted its existence. See his *"Lexicon Deutscher Schriftsteller"* vol. X. 1810.

8.   מסעות של רבי בנימן . נדפס בק"ק זולצבאך בשנת תקמ"ז .

Travels etc. printed at Sulzbach 542. (1782) small 8vo. 32 pp. square character.

A very poor reprint of L'Empereur's edition, upon wretched German blotting paper, full of mistakes and without the least literary value, being but a "popular sixpenny book."

9.   מסעות רבי בנימן . ואלקווא . . .

Travels of R. Benjamin. Printed at Zolkiew in Austrian Gallicia.

An edition quoted by the celebrated scholar, the Revd. Rabbi Salomon L. Rapoport, in his geographical preface to Shalom Cohen's Kore Haddoroth (Warsaw 1838). I have not been able to procure this reprint, which the Revd. Rabbi in a letter to me calls "a common edition," but which appears to contain some various readings. Several of these occur in the few quotations made use of in the above-mentioned preface, or rather essay, which, as well as all the other papers we possess from the pen of the Revd. Rabbi, prove him to be the first Hebrew scholar and critic of Europe. I am proud to say that both my translation and my notes have been enriched by his kind assistance, for which I here publicly render my best acknowledgments.

II. HEBREW AND LATIN

10.   מסעות של רבי בנימן ·

Itinerarium D. Benjaminis cum versione et notis Constantini L'Empereur ab Oppyck S. T. D. et S. L. P. in acad. Lugd. Batav. Lugd. Batavorum. Ex officina Elzeviriana. 1633. small 8vo. of 34 (unnumbered) and 234 (numbered) pages.

This edition, as far as the text and translation are concerned is composed of Nos. 4 and 12 of this list. The dissertation and the notes contain a vast deal of antiquated learning.

In his "Dissertatio ad Lectorem" L'Empereur speaks of Arias Montanus' translation in terms of contempt, but upon a nearer examination it will be found that L'Empereur made more mistakes than he ought to have done having such a translation before him. Renaudot's judgment of both editors cannot be called too severe; he says in speaking of the text: "Le Juif Benjamin . . . n'est pas un Auteur mesprisable, comme l'ont voulu faire croire quelques Sçavants qui ne l'ont pas entendu, à la teste desquels il faut mettre ceux qui entreprirent de le traduire, Arias Montanus, et après luy Constantin L'Empereur. Ils avoient travaillé l'un et l'autre, sur l'édition faite à Constantinople, qui estant un peu fautive, et assez peu nette, pouvoit embarasser ceux qui ne sçavaient pas la matiere. Arias Montanus fit des fautes énormes dans sa traduction, que le traducteur Hollandois n'a pas apperceües: et l'un et l'autre ayant mal leu plusieurs noms propres de villes, de peuples, et de provinces, en ont formé d'imaginaires qui ne furent jamais," and of the Notes: "A. Montanus a laissé à ses lecteurs le som de developper ces difficultez: mais L'Empereur, voulant esclaircir son Auteur, a joint à sa traduction, des notes chargées de citations Arabes et Hebraïques entierement inutiles. Car elles ne sont pas tirées des Escrivains originaux, ni des Geographes ou Historiens dont il ne connoissoit aucun, sinon la Geographie de Nubie, et Elmacin, que souvent il n'a pas entendus." *Anciennes Relations des Indes et de la Chine de deux Voyageurs Mahometans qui y allerent dans le neuviéme siecle; traduites d'Arabe: avec des Remarques sur les principaux endroits de ces Relations.* Paris 1718. Préface, pag. XXI. et XXII.

III. LATIN

11. Itinerarium Benjamini Tudelensis: in quo Res Memorabiles, quas ante quadringentos annos totum fere terrarum orbem notatis itineribus dimensus vel ipse vidit vel a fide dignis suae aetatis hominibus accepit, breviter atque dilucide describuntur; ex Hebraica Latinum factum Bened. Aria Montano Interprete.

Antwerpiae. ex officina Chr. Plantini
Archity pographi regii. MDLXXV.

The celebrated Arias Montanus was the first to introduce this work to the learned Christians, who, although they might understand the Scripture Hebrew, were strangers to that style, which is called the Rabbinic, and in which these travels are written. In many instances he has rather guessed at than faithfully translated the text, but not withstanding this, his labours deserve respect, and I have found his suggestions in many instances nearer the truth than those of later translators.

12. Itinerarium Benjaminis. Lat. redditum Lugd. Batav. 1633. 24mo.

This neat little volume, which forms part of the "Respublicae" is one of, if not *the* rarest of that series. The text is that of No. 10. of this list, and in consequence of its correctness and convenient form it has become a desideratum with students and collectors of books.

13. Itinerarium Benjaminis Tudelensis ex Versione Benedicti Ariae Montani. Subjectae sunt descriptiones Mechae et Medinae—Alnabi ex itinerariis Ludovicii Vartomanni et Johannis Wildii. Praefixa vero Dissertatio ad Lectorem, quam suae editioni praemisit Constantinus L'Empereur et nonnullae ejusdem notae. Helmstadi in typographeo Calixtino excudit Henningus Mullerus MDCXXXVI. small 8vo.

This little volume contains besides Montanus' translation the extracts mentioned in the above title. It is curious, although there is very little new matter in it. The editor having preferred Arias Montanus' to L'Empereur's version, has given a complete list of all the phrases in which these two translations differ, and in this book the student possesses *all* that had been written on the subject in Latin, down to the year of its publication.

14. Benjaminis Tudelensis Itinerarium ex Versione Benedicti Ariae Montani. Subjectae sunt Descriptiones Mechae et Medinae—Alnabi. Ex Itinerariis Ludovici Vartomanni et Johannis Wildii. Praefixa vero Dissertatio ad Lectorem, quam suae editioni praemisit Constantinus L'Empereur et nonnullae ejusdem Notae. Lipsiae apud Joann. Michael. Ludov. Teubner. MDCCLXIV. 8vo.

This is a corrected reprint of all the contents of the volume noticed just now under No. 13. The typography of this edition is infinitely superior to that of its predecessor.

IV. ENGLISH

15. The Peregrinations of Benjamin the Sonne of Jonas a Jew, written in Hebrew, translated into Latin by B. Arias Montanus. Discovering both the state of the Jews and of the world, about foure hundred and sixtie yeeres since.

For this first English translation see: Purchas' Pilgrims, London 1625, folio, vol. II. liv. 9. chap. 5. p. 1437. It is divided into five paragraphs.

16. The Travels of R. Benjamin, the Son of Jonas of Tudela, through Europe, Asia, and Africa, from Spain to China, from 1160 to 1173.

From the Latin versions of B. A. Montanus and Constantine l'Empereur, compared with other translations into different languages.

This extract of the Itinerary will be found in Harris' collection of voyages and travels. London 1744, 8. fol. vol. I. pp. 546 to 555, and the Introduction which is prefixed, as well as the Notes, are not devoid of interest. The editor treats (1) of the author of the work and of the several editions and translations of it; (2) of the objections that have been made to the credit of the author and the true state of the question; he then goes on to give an extract of the Itinerary and concludes by "Remarks and Observations on the foregoing Travels." The following note, which will be found at p. 554, letter g, will at once show the spirit of the editor: "It is very clear from a multitude of circumstances, that our author chiefly intended this work to celebrate his own nation, to preserve an account of the different places in which they were settled, and to do all in his power to keep up their spirits under their captivity, by putting them in mind of the coming of the Messiah. I must confess I consider this in a different light from most of the critics, for I do not conceive that a man's loving his countrymen ought to prejudice him in the opinions of his readers, and though it may possibly beget some doubts as to the fidelity of his relations with regard to the Jews, yet I do not see how this can with justice be extended to the other parts of this book." We very much regret that Mr. Harris neither understood Hebrew nor gave a complete translation of our author, as we have reason to believe that this would have made that part of the present edition superfluous, and would have gone far to reestablish the authority of the book.

[NOTE: *Number 16 is repeated by Asher in the 1840 edition.*]

16. Travels of Rabbi Benjamin, Son of Jonah of Tudela:

Through Europe, Asia, and Africa, from the ancient Kingdom of Navarre, to the frontiers of China. Faithfully translated from the Original Hebrew and enriched with a Dissertation and Notes, Critical, Historical, and Geographical. In which the true character of the author and intention of the work, are impartially (!) considered.

By the Rev. R. Gerrans, Lecturer of Saint Catherine Coleman, and Second Master of Queen Elisabeths Free Grammar-School, Saint Olave, Southwark.

This author, who flourished about the year 1160 of the Christian Era, is highly prized by the Jews and other admirers of Rabbinical learning; and has frequently been quoted by the greatest Orientalists that this, or any other, nation ever produced, but was never before (to the editors knowledge) wholly translated into English, either by Jew, or Gentile. London MDCCLXXXIV. 8vo.

The author of this edition pretends both on the title and in the course of the work, that he translated it "out of the Hebrew," and that his is "a most faithful translation," and this assertion has induced Dr. Chalmers in the Biographical Dictionary, and Mr. Lowndes in the Bibliographers Manual to state that this is really the case, but an examination of the work will clearly prove that Mr. Gerrans understood very little if anything of Hebrew, and that all his learning was derived from B. Arias Montanus, L'Empereur and Barratier. He denies having seen the latter work (quoted in No. 19) before he had printed the first chapters, but the very division into chapters, which is to be found in none of the originals and which was first introduced by Barratier proves the contrary, and the more strongly so as his and Montanus' chapters are exactly similar. The dissertation at the head of the work is a mere abridgement of Barratier's second volume, and those passages, which being Rabbinic and not understood, wrongly translated by Barratier, have been "faithfully" transcribed by Mr. Gerrans, and are in many instances complete nonsense. The following may serve as a specimen of Mr. Gerrans' critical tact and of his abilities as a translator. R. Benjamin, in speaking of the city of Lunel, mentions as usual several learned Jews; a Rabbi Asher, "very learned in the law."

„והוא חכם גדול בתלמוד והרב רבי משה גיסו, ורבי
שמואל החזן, ורבי שלמה הכהן״.

The literal translation of which runs as follows: ". . . and he is a great proficient in the Talmud, and (there are also) Rabbi Moshe his brother-in-law and R. Sh'muel the minister, and R. Sh'lomo Cohen (a descendant of Aaron)" Mr. Gerrans however translates: "This man is well skilled in the Talmudic writings. Here you likewise meet with that great R. Moses Gisso (!) and R. Samuel (Chasan), R. Salomon (13) the Priest," etc. In the note (13) he continues as follows: "He is commonly called by the Jews ש״י i.e. R. Salomon Jarchi (or rather Jerachi) from the city of Lunel which takes its name from Jareach, the Moon. . . . He died A.D. 1105, together with his disciple, who composed those prayers called מחזור or the circle, which contain many bitter invectives against Christians in general, and the Church of Rome in particular. This is one of Benjamins errors in chronology, for רשי was dead long before." There are almost as many errors as words in this passage! Gisso, his brother-in-law—he was ignorant enough to consider a proper name. Chasan (Minister), he explains in a note to be sometimes a reader and sometimes an executioner! Cohen—an appellation borne by the descendants of Aaron even to this day, he translates as priest. And to crown all, Mr. Gerrans accuses Benjamin of an error in chronology, because he was ignorant enough to suppose that by a certain R. Salomon Cohen, our author could have meant R. Salomon Jitschaki! It requires ignorance such as Mr. Gerrans alone could boast of to suppose anything of the kind, for (1) Rashi was no Cohen, and only the descendants of Aaron bear that appellation; (2) Rashi did not bear the appellation of Jarchi, although the initials of his name were thus explained by Buxtorff; (3) Rashi did not live at Lunel but at Troyes, or Luistre; (4) The מחזור (Machzor) or book of common prayer, the liturgy of the Jews, was composed many years before Rashi's time; (5) The Jews never dared to introduce any "bitter invectives" against the Church of Rome, and would have been very foolish to do so, as that church yielded them better protection than any other authority, and a man who could make mistakes of this kind dares to accuse Benjamin of ignorance, superstition, falsehood—the very basest of vices he can possibly imagine!

In the course of this translation we shall point out a few more of the grossest mistakes committed by Mr. Gerrans, and we consider this rather a duty, as his has been, unfortunately, for more than fifty years, the only edition accessible to the English public.

17. The Travels of R. Benjamin of Tudela from the Latin of B. Arias Montanus and Constantin L'Empereur compared with other Translations into different Languages.

This abridgement, which will be found in Pinkertons "General Collection of the best and most interesting Voyages and Travels of the world," London 1808—14. 4to. Vol. VII. contains such passages only as appear to have been of interest to the editor. Mr. Pinkerton concludes his extracts by stating, that one of the most remarkable things to be learned out of this work is the circumstance, that a person could travel so far at the time; he allows Rabbi Benjamin to have been an able judge of what he saw, and doubts not the veracity of the travels. Mr. Pinkerton has enriched this abridgment by some very valuable remarks, of which we shall avail ourselves in our volume of notes.

18. Voyage du celèbre Benjamin, au tour du monde, commencé l'an MCLXXIII (sic) contenant une exacte et succincte Description de ce qu'il a vû de plus remarquable, dans presque toutes les parties de la Terre; aussi bien que de ce qu'il en a apris de plusieurs de ses Contemporains dignes de foi. Avec un detail, jusques ici inconu, de la Conduite, des Sinagogues, de la Demeure et du Nombre des Juifs et de leurs Rabins, dans tous les endroits ou il a été etc. dont on aprend en même tems l'état où se trouvoient alors diférentes Nations avant l'agrandissement des Turcs.

Ecrit premierement en Hebreu par l'auteur de ce Voyage; traduit ensuite en Latin, par Benoit Arian Montan: et nouvellement du Latin en François. Le tout enrichi des Notes, pour l'explication de plusieurs passages.

The above title quoted at length informs the reader of the sources of this translation, which will be found to occupy 74 pages, 4to. of vol. I. in Bergeron's *Collection de Voyages, faits principalement en Asie, dans le* XII-XIII-XIV *et* XV *Siécles, a la Haye* 1735, 2 vols. 4to. The notes are of no value, nor is the map which accompanies this poor piece of work.

19. Voyages de Rabbi Benjamin fils de Jona de Tudele en Europe, en Asie et en Afrique depuis l'Espagne jusqu'à la Chine. Où l'on trouve plusieurs choses remarquables concernant l'Histoire et la Geographie et particulierement l'état des Juifs au douzième sie cle. Traduits de l'Hebreu et enrichis de notes et de Dissertations Historiques et Critiques sur ces Voyages. Par J. P. Barratier. Etudiant en Theologie. A. Amsterdam, aux dépens de la Compagnie. 1734. 2 vol. small 8vo.

Vol. I. contains the voyage and the notes. Vol. II. the eight dissertations mentioned in the title. With respect to the value of the work I can do no better than quote Gibbon's words (*Decline and Fall, chap.* LIII): "The Hebrew text has been translated into French by that marvelous Child Barratier, who has added a volume of crude learning"! It is hardly worth while here to enter into the question of whether young Barratier made the translation without the aid of some more experienced scholar, but it is to be regreted that even a child should have been biased by his teachers against all persons professing another creed than himself. From his notes it appears that the testimony of Roman Catholics and Jews were suspected by him because of their religious belief and it will be no difficult task to prove that his suspicions generally arise from ignorance only.

20. Voyages de Benjamin de Tudelle autour du monde commencé l'an 1173. De Jean du Plan-Carpin en Tartarie, du Frère Ascelin et de ses compagnons vers la Tartarie. De Guillaume de Rubruques en Tartarie et en Chine en 1253 suivi des Additions de Vincent de Beauvais et de l'Histoire de Guillaume de Naugès, pour l'Eclaircissement des precedentes Voyages. Paris, imprimé aux Frais du Gouvernement pour procurer du Travail aux ouvriers Typographes. Août 1830. in 8vo.

A reprint of No. 18, and curious only on account of the occasion, which procured Master Benjamin the honour of being called forth again from oblivion!

VI. DUTCH

21. De Reysen van R. Benjamin Jonas Tudelens. In de drie Deelen der Werelt. Int Nederduyts overgeschrieben door Jan Bara. Amsterdam, Jonas Rex. 1666. 24mo. 117 pp.

This translation having been made from L'Empereur's Latin version offers nothing new or valuable to the critical reader.

VIII. JEWISH-GERMAN

22.

דיזי זיין דיא רייזי פון רבי בנימן טודעלענס

רופא, וועלכי ער דורך דיא דרייא עקין פון דען עולם

גערייזט האט .

These are the voyages of R. Benjamin Tudelens the physician (!)
in which he has travelled through three corners of the world.
Amsterdam 451 (1691) 8vo.

This translation by Chaim Ben Jacob was made from
L'Empereur's text, and although the editor was a Jew, he was
too illiterate to correct any of the errors of L'Empereur, nor does
he pretend to any learning; but avows that he printed the book
merely as a popular treatise for the women and children of the
Dutch Jews, who speak a dialect of their own, mixed with German and Hebrew words.

23.

These are the Voyages, etc.   דיזי זיין דיא רייזי וכו' .

Frankfort on the Mainz, 471. (1711) 8vo.

A mere reprint of the former edition and consequently as
worthless in a critical point of view.

It is a curious fact that the Germans, who have written on every
subject and have translated almost everything from Aristotle to
Nicholas Nickleby, have no edition of these travels, nor have we
been able to trace any Swedish, Danish, Italian, or Spanish
translation.